SECRET SIGHTS II

D1382067

SECRET SIGHTS II

Unknown Medieval Ireland

Photographs and Text by

ROB VANCE

ashfield
PRESS

First published in 2005 by

ASHFIELD PRESS · DUBLIN · IRELAND

ISBN: 1 901658 43 0

A catalogue record for this book is available from the British Library.

Typeset by Ashfield Press in 12.5 on 16 point Dante
Designed by
SUSAN WAINE

Printed in Ireland by
ßETAPRINT LIMITED, DUBLIN

Frontispiece:
Moone High Cross, Co. Kildare,
The Flight into Egypt, c. 9th century.

Contents

Acknowledgments

Yet again I find myself in humble admiration of the historians and archaeologists of Medieval Ireland upon whose work this book is based. Their patient years of research appear similar in many ways to the monks who toiled in the scriptoria, turning darkness into light in order to reveal what they understood as truth. I hope today's scholars find a just reward in *this* life. The bibliography is a tribute to those who have worked in what in many ways is an challenging field of Irish history, fraught with issues of culture, religion and identity, and frequently oppositional to the orthodoxy of popular 'Irishness'. Access to that part of Ireland's past is difficult and fragmentary and I salute their doggedness and refusal to accept contemporary mythology as fact.

My son Jocelyn assisted in taking the pictures, as did (young) Kevin McGilligan. To both, I offer my thanks. Jim Butler and Paddy Deery of Repro 35 supervised the processing and scanning of the images and, as before, they provided great service and perfect quality. To John Davey, Judith Elmes and Susan Waine of Ashfield Press a special thanks for their patience, creativity and attention to detail. My agent, Jonathan Williams, as always, provided calm during stormy moments. Dr John Bradley of NUI Maynooth deserves special mention as he kindly read the manuscript and his comments and advice kept this wayward scholar from many errors of judgement.

At RTE Cork, researchers Aoife O'Callaghan and Joe Howard, Fil Carson of finance, and head of production Colm Crowley were supportive throughout the filming of 'Secret Sights II' and I was fortunate again to have a superb creative team for the nine weeks on the road. To director Peter Carr and producer Marie Toft, my appreciation for all your work and profuse apologies for fluffing my lines (occasionally). To Brendan Cahill, who patiently provided the location sound, and Barry Donnelan, whose 'eye' gave such a lift to the images, thanks to you both.

And special credit is due to Will Harris, who was responsible for my work being seen on television in the first place.

13th century arrow loop in Ferns Castle, Co. Wexford.

Introduction

ALTHOUGH THE MEDIA has been my constant career, Irish history has been my quiet passion. Possibly by virtue of Huguenot, Irish and Norman ancestry, it was inevitable that curiosity about the past would be part of my character. Of all three cultural strands, one has always been uppermost. Since childhood, my distant O'Fogarty forbears have been tugging at my innermost thoughts as if seeking expression, and it is through bringing Irish history to a wider audience that I may do them some small honour.

I studied History at Avoca School under the late and gifted Dr John de Courcy Ireland; his charm and insight made that subject alive in a way few teachers could match. Although I attended third-level for brief spans of time in my late teens, it was considerably later in life before Irish Nationalism and its influence on identity and cultural expression became the subject of both my MA and subsequent MPhil with the Universities of Sheffield and UWE Bristol respectively. But taking pictures, still or moving, has always held an enthralment that only occasionally dipped below obsession. I would like to think it is more under control today.

From the electronic viewpoint of the 21st century, the medieval world is a distant and convoluted era, a time when piety alternated with violent chaos. Yet, surprisingly perhaps, those 1,000 years from 500 to 1500 AD contain similarities to today.

14th century grave slab, Athassel Priory, Co. Kilkenny.

9

Then, Christianity was the great cement that held it all together, and while it bound the great majority to poverty and deference to their betters, it alleviated the misery of the sick and poor and pricked the conscience of the rich. Above the Church, the great Gaelic and Old English nobles of Ireland, equivalent to today's multi-millionaires, were occasionally benevolent but generally they focussed on the job in hand: more land, more money, more of everything. At that time, authority in Ireland rested on the complex interaction between chiefs and vassals, tributes and taxes. By the later Middle Ages, England had become the distant overlord, claiming jurisdiction without equality, while, in general, the native Irish lords insisted on personal independence without national responsibility.

Society today is held together by a more elastic adhesive than religious belief, and in theory, at least, anyone can become as wealthy as a medieval Gaelic lord. They can certainly live like one. Unlike medieval Ireland, political power is now more diffuse and seems, on the surface at least, to be democratically accountable. Whether the rich today are more benevolent or less avaricious and whether or not Brussels is the secular Rome is debatable. Then, as now, we as individuals are reflections of the society we create and our idealisation of capitalism may be as much a wilful mis-recognition of its reality as any devout pilgrim's hope of salvation through grace.

But if this were a book on the medieval history of England or France, it would begin in a cathedral or a sainted abbey, atmospheric with history. I could walk its gilded nave, photograph the sarcophagi of the great and the good, recumbent effigies of those who had led the land through its wars and ultimately created the past out of which the present grew. In the 13th-century cathedral of Christ Church in Ireland's capital city, however, no Irish kings lie beneath royal tombs nor any Gaelic queens who built nunneries or helped the poor. No captains of their nations who fought Ireland's wars are buried in state, nor are there gilded inscriptions in our ancient language which tell of Irish kings hammering the Sassenachs. But the Irish kings and the nobility fought; bravely, foolishly in many ways,

The stone font of the now vanished monastery of Clonard, Co. Meath.

for they refused to compromise, their great pride blinding them to the reality of medieval politics, where only the most powerful or cunning could survive. Medieval Ireland was the bear pit where lumbering, slow-moving old ways were torn to pieces by the mastiffs of power politics and the money economy. Ireland was where the old met the new in a sordid tale without a happy ending. What happened in the Middle Ages is the story behind this book.

MARRE HYBERBOR

Ebuda   Eb

62

·19·

61

60

Venicuiu   Rhobog
boreū   udia   diuiu pm
pmo   fl   Rhogrodu
Herpe   fl
rauig   ditaui   Togia fl
fl
Clariui

Magiata   Regia   uidoris

libius fl   Vlinai   ifaniu

HIB
ERN
Magiata Iela   Bubinda fl
te   Ebaui
Regia   Laberos
aliera   Eblana   Adra
Ansoba fl   Cauy
Sinus fl Autini   IA
obera fl   Linnos
Gangani   Macoli   Manapij
cum   moduing fl
duris fl   dunu manapi
ta
Velabri   iernis   Coriudi
fl   bir   Satz
iernis fl   Iernis   Voie   gus   pmot
fl
iberm   Brigauis   Mona
Notum
pmont.

59

58

Lag
Prīc

Tiso

OCEANVS OCCIDENTALIS

Tun

Leue

Beginnings

WHEN PEOPLE TALK about Irish history, certain dates and events are seen as more important than others. Most Irish people have some idea that long ago Brian Ború was good and, later, Oliver Cromwell was bad. And if they have a lingering sense of shame about the Famine, then its converse, an assertive pride about 1916 and Irish Independence would probably summarise the emotive elements of popular history.

The parallel belief that people in Ireland are descended from European Celts is an important part of popular imagination. It is the unconscious assumption behind much of Irish Nationalism, but in archaeological terms, it lacks conclusive evidence. That may sound inconsistent, in that it is a widely held belief, but in terms of what is required to provide a credible and satisfying ancestry for a nation, Celtic Ireland is difficult to find. What remains of the civilisation from the pre-Christian era is fragmentary and obscured beneath origin myths and legends. In reality, 'Celtic' is a linguistic term only.

In historical terms, the marauding Keltoi of Greek nightmare became recognised as Celts only in the mid-19th century owing (primarily) to excavations in Switzerland and later Germany and the subsequent reclassification of what had been seen as barbarian darkness. In that distant time, most of Europe was

Map of Ireland, 2nd century AD according to Ptolemy of Alexandria, published in Rome in 1490

13

'Celtic' in the sense of a shared culture of varying degree. The descriptions of a wild, fair-haired people fond of poetry, fighting and general mayhem are numerous, especially in the commentaries of the Celts' military adversaries, the Romans. The discrepancies, however, between the rich and bejewelled European Celtic nobility and the meagre spoils of Britain, and especially Ireland, suggest that the heartland of the Celts lay between the Danube and the Rhine, and not the Hill of Tara and the River Shannon.

That said, Ireland is an old place and antiquity presses in on all sides, sometimes overburdened with recent memory, sometimes curiously empty, as if cleansed and purified by some agent. Although the popular sites need protection from sheer numbers, my personal preference is for the eerie charm of the unknown ruin. There, personal subjectivity is given free rein and medieval vaults and echoing footsteps create their own gothic narrative.

BEGINNINGS

The earliest traces of habitation, date from c.7000 BC, when fishermen and their families lived off the rich mussel-bearing mud and abundant oysterbeds of the Antrim coast, dumping their shells to be rediscovered as middens. These Mesolithic rubbish heaps later gave valuable information about their lives and diets. Later arrivals created the megalithic culture which lasted for millennia, evolving into different, and in many cases something approaching artistic, shapes, as taste and function seem to have adapted and morphed into the beginnings of symbolic expression.

Looking at these mute monuments, one is struck by the feeling that a pile of stones so erected came to have meaning and especially so since some were decorated with symbols that could suggest planetary movements. Eventually the later stone circles became the route to transcendence, as ritual moved from the great interior shrines of Newgrange and the Boyne to an exterior and communal rite. Solitary standing stones, phallic perhaps but in some cases burial sites and especially wetland depositions of weapons, denotes the emergence of an armed elite, capable of defining and certainly defending territory. To do so required a sense of identity or difference and the wish to subjugate others. By around 1200 BC these new groupings and their new technology of metalworking left the great tombs obsolete as status symbols if still worthy of reverence. The Bronze Age is a period rich in gold ornaments relating to dress and probably authority. The early gold lunulae and later torcs indicate a change in status from giant boulder tombs of prosperous farmers to elegant earrings and necklaces, symbols of power and affluence for a mining aristrocracy. By the early Christian centuries (c. 200-300 AD) a new land was emerging from the obscurity of pre-history.

While it is true to say that art and metalwork of both early and later Christian Ireland [c. 600 & 1200 AD] is Celtic in design and inspiration, it does not prove that Celts as a distinct population grouping had arrived or were living on the island at that time. The metalwork and manuscripts merely show that (Irish) craftsmen were highly skilled in the popular motifs of the era as different uses of decorative foliage and animals for script and sword travelled backwards and forwards across Scandinavia, Anglo-Saxon Britain and Ireland. What does prove the 'Celtic' roots of those early peoples is the language they spoke, although there is little archaeological evidence for a rich Celtic aristocracy on this island in the centuries preceding Christianity.

As to how the island moved from being an underpopulated and agriculturally primitive outpost of Europe to a land capable of developing a system of laws, land-owners and a thriving cross-channel piracy business, no one has a clear answer. Ptolemy's map of the 2nd century AD suggests various tribes living on the island and these may have been refugees from Roman Gaul, traders on coastal settlements or branches of existing Belgic or otherwise Britannic tribes, derivative of European Celts of earlier centuries.

It would appear, however, that from the 3rd century onwards, development began across a wide range of activities from agriculture

to social organisation, and since folk movements across the Irish Sea had always been a regular part of the life of these islands, much of Munster's prosperity certainly, may have been due to their returning emigrants. It is their knowledge enriched from centuries of contact with Roman Britain who proudly formed the elite in some parts of pre-Viking Ireland.

Of the many assumptions about cultural identity, language and its expression through literature is one of the defining elements and Ireland has had a tradition since the 17th century of a literature in English. But it is from the earliest times that the richest Gaelic tradition emerges. Irish was certainly the language of the island before Christianity and was originally an Indo-European language, spoken in many dialects across Bronze-Age Europe. We are fortunate that an extraordinary collection of vivid tales in Old-Irish was collected by Christian monks from the 6th and 7th centuries onward and thankfully, not overly Christianised, as happened in Wales in a later period. In reading these bizarre tales of head-hunting, great feasts and chariot warfare, one might assume they were first and foremost *of this*

island and nowhere else and that the landscape and locations described were part and parcel of a glorious, if overgrown, Celtic past. But the elements of the most famous tale, even though scholars have suggested the route of the epic through the countryside, are in their source Indo-European. The *Táin Bo Cuailigne* (The Cattle Raid of Cooley), while having a superficial resemblance to the Trojan Wars, has, in one episode, the hero

The Skelligs rock, home to monks from the 7th century to the 10th and one of Europe's most remote hermitages.

Adam and Eve, on the 12th century gable wall of Ardmore Church, Co Waterford, founded by St Declan in the 5th century.

The bank of the massive ring-fort at Rathurles, Co Tipperary, by tradition the ancient seat of the O'Kennedys of Tipperary.

Cuchulainn defeating and beheading three sons of Nechta Scene, itself a variation on an Indo-European initiatory myth. Other similarities occur in Roman literature when the mythical Curiatii are defeated by Horatius and in Indian literature when the three-headed son of Tvastar is defeated by Aptya. [Laing, 1995] Like the inhabitants of the island, the tales themselves may have many authors and origins.

But this is a book about Medieval Ireland and broadly speaking, it is a period of written history. It is the time when Irish history enters modern life as it gathers pace towards the defeat of Gaelic Ireland at the Battle of Kinsale. It is unfortunate that much of the written information comes from the opponents of Ireland, whose viewpoint resembles Conquistadors writing about the

Indian tribes of Peru or Mexico. The colonial narratives are almost unaware of their arrogance, as if ignorant of their often intrusive and violent warping of Ireland's somewhat wayward developmental trajectory. There is no doubt, however, that the leaders produced from Ireland's chieftains and kings were, in the main, ineffective and locally focussed. From today's perspective, they lacked a sense of nation, but there was no nation in the modern-day sense to be aware of at that time.

During the late 1500s, Ireland provided plenty of excuses for England's interference, allying itself with Spain in the cause of the Counter-Reformation without being united within itself. The country was punished militarily, economically and spiritually, in the sense of having its will to resist shattered and its wealth ultimately placed in the hands of a minority, whose immediate interest was in personal enrichment rather than in seeing the country prosper. It was the 18th century before a sense of political nationhood was to emerge, its mood alternating in agreement with revolutionary America and France.

ARCHITECTURE

Irish 'architecture' really begins with the early Christian churches and hermitages but most were in wood, the size determined by the Brehon laws as 4.6 x3 m [15x10ft]. Timber structures do not survive centuries of damp or war, but later stone churches, such as the 9th-century Gallarus Oratory in County Kerry probably reflect their timber forerunners in proportion. [Harbison, 1978] [Leask ,1955]

As in Europe, architecture was an outlet for religious belief and artistic expression. Romanesque architecture came to Ireland through enlightened nobles such as Cormac MacCarthy of Cashel, who in 1127 chose an eclectic mixture of German, French and English motifs for his chapel at Cashel in County Tipperary. This style was repeated in further religious buildings. Gothic Cathedrals were begun in Dublin, Waterford Limerick and Kilkenny in the late 12th and early 13th centuries and these immense buildings with their spires and battlements

The island monastery of Inismurray off the Sligo coast, plundered by the Vikings in the 9th century.

reminded peasants and merchants alike that secular and spiritual power were never far apart. Buildings, however, have little history in themselves. It is the stories of the people who built or inhabited the structures that give the stones 'flesh and blood', and the buildings illustrated in the book have stories and often a contentious past. Fortunately, portions of the architecturally rich medieval landscape still exist across Ireland, an immense open-air warehouse of styles and fashions in brick and stone, from walled towns to richly endowed friaries. This is the photographic terrain of *Secret Sights II*.

The Rock of Cashel for centuries, home to Munster's kings and bishops.

Outside the cities and towns, Ireland was a series of large and small independent fiefdoms, small kingdoms where both Gaels and *Anglais* endowed abbeys and friaries and built

castles large and small for comfort and defence, the architectural styles varying according to taste and wealth.

Walled cities and towns were established by the Normans often on what had been coastal Viking trading ports. Across the country especially in the south and rural hinterland, they often centred on the castle of the dominant lord. The towns were granted Charters, a type of 'duty free' status which gave them immunity from some types of Gaelic or Anglo-Irish taxation. The more prosperous traded with the Gaelic hinterland, formed guilds, held Corpus Christi festivals similar to those in Spain today, and led a life of relative comfort, watching the English and the Irish outside the walls dispute with each other while vying for the trade and advantage of both.

The abbeys and friaries of the Augustinians, Benedictines and others were strongly influenced by their original houses in England or France. In the west of Ireland, Gaelic foundations tended to be of a more modest size in comparison to the churches of Kilkenny, Tipperary and Meath. Architecture in Ireland evolved as society changed and Ireland had times when church building was vigorous and healthy and later times when it declined. The 14th, century for example, was a lengthy time of decline in the colony owing to plague, famine, war and the political indifference of England.

Following the discovery of America by Columbus in 1492, Ireland found itself in the path of Spain and its growing empire. To English eyes, Ireland, if controlled by Spain, would in turn control the Atlantic approaches – and it is only because of fear of Spanish control that the conquest of Ireland took shape in the later 16th century. In response to these un settled times, Irish architecture becomes exemplified in the tower houses, typical fortified dwellings of Irish lords from the 15th century onwards.

WRITTEN HISTORY

Realistically, medieval Ireland begins some centuries before the Norman invasion, a time when what we call Celtic Ireland still retained the manners and customs of unchanging tradition. It was a time before the Vikings had established their trading ports, the forerunners of most of the later cities. The monks, who were the protohistorians of the 8th and 9th centuries, attempted to regularise the random and miscellaneous events of earlier times into a narrative and probably removed items that didn't conform to their wish for a coherent story. This early wish for history to be clean and tidy is similar to how Irish history was rewritten from the late 19th century onwards as 'a struggle over 800 years to rid the country of foreigners'. Much of the work of monks and especially later national polemicists became 'tradition' and acquired a degree of authority that has stood as a barrier to understanding what happened in the early centuries of the Christian era and the later medieval period. The nationalist histories of the 19th and 20th centuries continue to offer a rich terrain for textual exploration, suffused like the *Tain Bo Cuailigne* with mythology, heroes, blood sacrifice and an obsession with territorial sovereignty.

The locations and characters mentioned in earlier mythology, however, provide a tantalising glimpse of a pagan land, but it might not be Ireland; it could be the Iron Age equivalent of Middle Earth. And while the Irish language is an indication of remote ancestry, Ireland's ancient tongue is as likely to have been carried by culture and commerce as by Aryan warriors from Iberia or Gaul. Early Christian Ireland, however, does provide an imaginary territory to believe in, an ancestral homeland before the foreigner came, but its terrain, etched with high crosses, holy wells and saints' meanderings, is really a substitute for a missing Celtic Ireland.

Britannia was the Roman province invaded by the Angles, Jutes, and Saxons who defeated the British, gradually confining them to the area we call Wales. The chronicler Bede makes the point that the island of Britain was inhabited by four peoples: British, English, Pictish and Irish. Gradually, understanding and scholarship of that obscure time is coming to light, defining in a different way who 'the Irish' are in terms of traditional cultural modes. Ideas about the Irish will change, but while important levels of debate exist about nationality

rather than nationalism in certain quarters of Irish academia, it has yet to reach the streets or the popular media.

A medieval king on the gable wall of the Chapel Royal at Dublin Castle said to represent Brian Boru.

CULTURAL EXPRESSION

At present, it appears that we are left with relatively few idioms of expression for the Irish history of the Middle Ages, a relatively recent era in the ancestry of the people of the island. There are few contemporary texts to explain that period from the Irish side, and the English manuscripts are generally unflattering. At present, medieval Ireland, while subject to increasing academic exploration, is not yet readily accessible as an artistic or cultural resource.

In visual terms, the example that sufficed as 'Ancient Irish Art' for most of the 20th century was the extraordinary gospel bestiary from the Christian manuscripts. That scrolling foliate artwork, while being a mixture of La Tène motifs abandoned centuries before on continental Europe, was enriched in Ireland by Anglo-Saxon animal interlace but ultimately developed by native genius. Another and more recently adopted source of inspiration has been the Stone Age spirals from thousands of years before anything remotely Celtic. Perhaps in a secular age, the Newgrange triple spiral motif seems more appropriate than the Book of Kells as a source of corporate 'Irishness'.

Another expression of culture from the Middle Ages has been music. From figures representing King David with a harp, on Durrow High Cross, Derrick's Images of Ireland (1581) showing pipers and even Giraldus mentions music. A combination of song and dance developed into many outlets, including the recent phenominally successful 'Riverdance' itself replacing the Clancy Brothers ensemble of the 1960s-1980s..

But that rich and complex world of Medieval Ireland exists, closer by centuries in time, nearer in language and custom than any 'Celtic' era, and I argue that it is more real a template for the Irish as a people than the imaginary Celtic Ireland of centuries before. It remains largely unknown and we appear to have no home-grown Wars of the Roses, no Great Plagues, no Chaucer or Shakespeare to

Swords Castle, built around 1200 as a palace for the Archbishops of Dublin, was modified in the 14th century to provide a Great Hall for banquets, and houses for the Constable and other important functionaries. It is at present being restored by the Office of Public Works.

tell us of life in the Irish Middle Ages. Unlike England, there is no 'Age of Kings'. It is like a history book with pages torn out.

At one level, the reason why Ireland lacked chronicles was a dearth of patrons. The O'Briens and O'Conor's were such people, but they were rare. What was recorded, in the correspondence of the Dublin administration to its overseers in London was often the point of view of the stranger looking at a foreign land that spoke a strange language, a stranger whose presumption of superiority coloured the narrative, but revealed his own truth. When the compass allowed Europe to access the benefits of conquest abroad, Ireland's geographic position

meant that this island was in the contested path of the empire-building nations of Spain and England. We became part of European 'History'.

Storming of a walled town.
[*Knights Engravings of Old England*, 1845.]

MEDIEVAL IRELAND AND NATIONS

Medieval Ireland has often been presented as a clash of two systems, mutually antagonistic and incomprehensible. This was not the case. It was not that simple. While the Normans in Connacht were indistinguishable from their Gaelic relations, those inside the Pale retained a more 'English' outlook. Ulster remained centuries behind in its continuation of ancient traditions, while Munster managed a juggling act between two legal systems, primogeniture and gavelkind, the inheritance by eldest male and the fratricidal competition of tanistry. [Nicholls, 1973]

Castleroche commands a pass into south Armagh on the medieval route northwards from Dundalk. It was built c. 1236 by Lady Rohesia de Verdon and improved and enlarged by her son John who added a Great Hall with window seats. [Leask, 1955]

Detail from the tomb of Saidbh Macmurrogh Kavanagh,one of the many Gaelic princesses who married into the ruling Norman-Irish elite in the middle-ages.She was buried in the Butler endowed church of Gowran, Co. Kilkenny.

The thirteenth century St Laurences's Gate, which defended the main entrance to the medieval town of Drogheda, site of many meetings of the Irish Parliament during that era.

The normal view of Irish history, excluding the Middle Ages, is understandable to a degree, because it was a confusing and complex period that lacked 'Irish' records to reflect the indigenous position. Nevertheless, the churches, abbeys and castles indicate that the parochially focussed Gaelic aristocracy had a degree of sophistication, sharing similar attitudes to their counterparts elsewhere in Europe. Unfortunately, in many ways, they also shared their fate – that of small, weak, principalities in the orbit of a colonial power. In as much as Mexico and Peru were Spanish colonial experiments, Ireland was England's laboratory, the place where she learned the colonial game.

But there were other nations involved in the beginnings of that competition and Scotland, initially, was the most sympathetic to Ireland's position.

The Scots were a combination of several races that had evolved roughly into two main groupings by the 11th century.

Firstly, there was the dynasty based in Central Scotland, descended from the line of Fergus Mac Eirc, which became the dominant Scottish royal house. It gradually moved its focus from Celtic affairs to Anglo-Saxon and then Norman as their own forays brought them land in the borderlands and Cumbria. Although the Irish annalists assumed a Celtic connection to these Scottish kings, by the 12th century it was becoming attenuated as Norman England was growing in power and Scottish royal attention was focussed on matters southerly. However, Robert and Edward Bruce would reassert this sense of collective identity in the 14th century.

The Northern province of Moray was the territory for the second Scottish dynasty. It was here the descendants of Loarn Mac Eirc, hemmed in by Scotto-Pictish rivals to the south and east, produced kings like Findlaech Mac Ruaidri, the father of Macbeth, known as MacBethad to the Irish chroniclers. This line was related to Leinster families through intermarriage, but the fascinating connection may be in the 'Barrow' group of Stone Crosses, influenced by Pictish and Scandinavian artwork, which lie within that ancient kingdom of Leinster. The idea of picture crosses may have developed in Ireland in the 9th century under the influence of the Céli Dé (people of God), an ecclesiastical reform movement. While the crosses are not directly related to sites associated with this reform movement, they were probably the impetus behind the intellectual and liturgical revival of the 9th century. [de Paor, 1958]

In a broader sense, the distant medieval period is at variance with what has become 'official Ireland', a place where rural simplicity has become the touchstone of authentic 'Irishness'. Up to the 19th century, 'The Irish People', depending on the subject, meant either the Anglo-Irish landowning gentry, the farming class or the Catholic middle classes. The great mass of illiterate peasants, in Ireland as in Europe did not really have a history, nor were they an audience. Few were interested in their welfare. These Irish people, in a nationalist sense, had not been invented before about 1860. They briefly appear as the croppies of 1798, the supporters of Daniel O'Connell in the

1820s and as the doomed emigrants of 1845-50. Because many of those who remained continued to speak Irish, they ultimately became the chosen archetypes for true 'Irishness' in the Irish state after Independence. Perhaps the complex world of Medieval Gaelic Ireland was too high a culture for the inverted snobbery of the emerging state.

Whatever about the shortcomings of the rural Ireland of folk memory, ordinary people in medieval life certainly had few rights, no voice and were illiterate. There was nothing to read anyway. But to get a realistic picture of Medieval Ireland, the easiest comparison is with contemporary Medieval Europe, a disparate collection of semi-feudal lordships, with brutal and power-hungry rival nobilities fighting to the death as in 15th-century Italy. In Ireland, however, the penalty and outcome for similar vendettas was often dependent on a wildly partisan monarchy. Irish national sentiment waxed and waned during those turbulent years, but in general it was local self-interest more than any 'National' self-awareness which bound together Irish lords and their European colleagues.

In a popular sense, the architecturally rich and culturally diverse world of medieval Ireland is somewhat alien and perhaps uncomfortable. It can be disturbing, in present-day political terms, to find that the apparently *opposed* Gaelic and English were in many circumstances united, while England's allies were as often to be found in supposed 'Irish' families and their leaders. Medieval Ireland was certainly a place of intermittent anarchy, and the loyalty of Irish princes and chieftains was more often allied to various monarchs of England than any notion of an independent 'state'. Irish dynasts had little sense of a territorial nation and, in general, their conflicts with the growing power of Tudor and Elizabethan England were unfocussed, opportunist and ultimately ineffective. The final irony of late medieval or (more properly) early modern history is that while Oliver Cromwell is infamous for his massacre of the inhabitants of Drogheda and Wexford, Catholic as they were, his reason – that they were Royalist supporters of Charles II – is forgotten, as is the fact that the majority were descendants of Norman and Elizabethan planters, not the Gaelic Irish.

IDENTITY

Ireland, in a way, never got to the starting blocks of sovereignty, never began that collective sense of identity that shaped the English monarchy on which the Gaelic and *Anglais* relied intermittently for support. It lacked an Irish 'Royal Family' with the accompanying civil service hub and administrative spokes that went with its power. The system of the local king being ruler, judge and general meant a concentration of power in an individual, and a subsequent reduction in the ministers of state who normally surrounded European and English monarchy. And that institution of monarchy had its own gravitational 'pull' – towards the centre. But for Irish kings and chieftains, the giving of obedience and the acknowledging of authority to the highest of high kings, the 'Ard-Ard-Rí' on another island was never going to happen without military control. But in Ireland there was nowhere to control, no centre of power. From Ireland's perspective, the imaginary centre of power in London could never hold.

Ireland was certainly different from England at that time. It has been described as tribal, suggesting lands held in communal ownership or organised in clans, as in Scotland But the Irish chieftains and kings formed family groups, *derbfine*, comprising grandfather, sons and grandsons, and it was the 'king' of the family group who decided the distribution of their territorial land and what rent should be paid. The Irish tribes were no more tribal than the Hapsburgs, Plantagenets or Windsors. Tribal was a term useful in a context of implied lack of title to land, for if the land was held communally, then no one had ownership, no one had title.

In one important aspect, Irish regal succession differed form that of England and Europe The tanistry laws, appearing first in the medieval period, offered a limited form of succession through election from the *derbfine*. This allowed a choice, so that idiots and chil-

33

dren could not succeed to a position encompassing king, judge and general. Feudal law insisted on primogeniture, whereby the eldest succeeds, irrespective of ability or inclination. Although Irish tanistry frequently involved feuds and small wars, land was secondary to cattle in the calculation of wealth. But from the Normans' point of view, land was the one possession that nobody could have enough of. It was what they wanted and what the Irish had. It gave the owner the most return for the least labour and its ownership brought power to those who owned it. From the dawn of the Middle Ages, land-owners were law-makers and the Church and the power of the State stood behind them. Much of Ireland's medieval history is the attempt of strong kings and chieftains to take land from weaker members of the same caste. The Normans and Elizabethans followed the same custom, using however, the force of 'law' to obtain their ends. In the thousand years from the fall of the Roman Empire to the rise of Renaissance Italy, Ireland underwent its own decline and fall, but through that fall, a new society emerged, painfully and with great difficulty. The Ireland that had to regrow itself after the Battle of Boyne is the Ireland of today.

Roman and Early
Medieval Ireland

THIS PART OF HISTORY may seem irrelevant to Medieval Ireland, but the roots of that era begin in early Christian Ireland, a time arguably linked with the collapse of Roman Britain. During that broad era, the country appears to have undergone a considerable transformation in farming and organisation and St. Patrick himself may have been the later iconic emblem of an intrusive military grouping from Roman Britain. This is not such a wild, idiosyncratic assertion as it seems and I hope to show in this short chapter that much of what were the origins of so-called 'Celtic Ireland' may have been anything but Celtic, in a purist sense. The society out of which Medieval Ireland emerged appears more Roman than La Tène or Halstatt, the European categories for Celtic artefacts and artwork. Indeed, the first map of Ireland was that of Ptolemy, who in the 2nd century AD identified headlands, tribes and other features suggesting knowledge of the country derived from trading or perhaps military contacts.

In AD 406, a coalition of Vandals, Alans and Germanic tribes crossed the frozen Rhine and entered an unprotected Gaul. The Roman army had been withdrawn to defend Italy from the Visigoths and the legions left in Britain were quickly brought across the English Channel to defend the Empire. Rome itself was sacked in 410. The Empire had existed for so long that no one

Ferns Castle, built around 1200 by William Marshall, who succeeded to MacMurrough-Kavanagh lands by right of his wife Isabella, daughter of Strongbow and Aoife.

could imagine an alternative and when Rome came under the control of Alaric the Visigoth, he wished the Empire to continue. Britain was forgotten and left to its own devices. It was invaded by Angles, Saxons, Frisians and Jutes, who established a permanent settlement in the south-east by 450.

Romans such as Tacitus and Agricola were both aware of Ireland. Tacitus states that while Agricola was campaigning along the north-west coast of Britain, he came upon an Irish chief who, it appears, had been driven from his kingdom by a rebellion. The identity of this chief is not definitive but may have been Tuathal Techmar, whose disputed death is recorded as being around AD 106. Theories about Techmar's return with Roman mercenaries have an unfortunate parallel with Dermot MacMurrough's use of the Normans a millennium later. The Irish Sea was always a medium for cultural and political exchange as when the English royal family fled after 1066 and found shelter with the MacMurrough's, who launched two invasions of England in an effort to restore them.

OVERVIEW

According to orthodox archaeology, the Romans failed to invade Ireland or to influence it to any great degree. Accepted academic opinion believes that there was a Roman presence on the island but that it was small, linked primarily to trade and of little cultural significance. This viewpoint is traditional but it appears to contradict what is there in the ground. The extensive coin hoards showing the heads of Roman emperors of the 1st and 2nd centuries AD are an example of the contentious nature of 'Roman Ireland' being claimed by one group of academics as 19th-century misplacements, and by others as evidence of occupation and settlement.

A further anomaly lies with Newgrange and Tara, two of the oldest and most significant Irish sites relating to a public sense of who the Irish are. Both are associated in a general way with some deep Irishness relating to tribal Celts and ancient structures. But the curious thing about Tara, for all its significance in literature, is that no relevant *Celtic* material has been discovered on the site. According to Professor Barry Raftery and others, what has been found suggests settlers or traders from Roman Britain, not Celts from the Rhineland. Another famous 'Celtic' site, Uisneach in County Westmeath, had 4th-century

Roman coins and a curious Roman key, paralleled by a pad-lock found at Tara, both suggesting wealth and the need to secure possessions, reflecting a radically different society to the general Irish model existing at the time. Again, no native material was found along with the Roman coins, suggesting that the Roman material was not cash belonging to Irish traders or pirates but part of the wealth of Roman settlers, or at least long-established traders.

The Romans in Britain were aware of Ireland, perhaps in the first instance as a remote and exotic tourist destination, because Newgrange was found to be strewn with Roman coins from the 1st to the 5th centuries, deposited more than likely as tokens by the Romano-British equivalent of tourists or pilgrims.

Hard evidence suggests that Lambay Island, off the coast of north County Dublin, shows the earliest Romano-British arrivals. The burials discovered during building work were from the 1st and 2nd centuries AD and were probably Brigantes, a Celtic grouping from Britain familiar with Roman culture, who may have fled the

Roman military campaigns of AD 71 by coming to Hibernia, as this island was known abroad. Another set of burials was accidentally unearthed by workers building the railway around Bray Head in the early 19th century, dispersed and not properly recorded, unfortunately. These individuals seem to have had Roman coins placed on their eyes, as was usual for citizens of the Empire who wished to pay the ferryman across the river of death, the Styx. Further evidence of settlement was found later in the century in the vicinity of Stonyford, Co. Kilkenny. There, in a classic Roman cremation burial of the 1st or early 2nd century, the ashes were contained in a glass cinerary urn that had been sealed with a polished bronze disc-mirror. The glass urn was accompanied by a small glass bottle, possibly a cosmetic-holder, suggesting the burial of a woman. Burials of this nature are more likely with a permanent Roman presence than would be explained merely by occasional trading contacts. The area south of Freestone Hill in County Kilkenny has many Roman sites, as was detailed in *Secret Sights* [Gill &

Prow of a Roman galley, perhaps similar to those used for trade on the Irish Sea c. 1st to 5th century AD.

Macmillan, 2002] Richard Warner of the Ulster Museum suggests that this location, not far from Waterford Harbour, could point to the possible existence of a Roman trading station in the area.

Finally, Drumanagh, close to Loughshinny in north County Dublin is a promontory fort of great potential significance and perhaps the most contentious 'Roman' site in Ireland. Bounded by vertical cliffs on three sides, this extensive promontory of some 40 acres in area is defended by three closely spaced ramparts of earth with intervening ditches. In the 1970s, a shard of 1st-century Gallo-Roman Samian ware was recovered from deep soil on the promontory. Another later discovery of two 2nd-century Roman coins occurred near the fort, and during the 1980s the ploughing of ancient pastureland in the vicinity turned up piece after piece of Gallo-Roman pottery, which appears to have been deliberately kept from academic discussion or public debate by the National Museum. Further random findings of pottery on surrounding farmland have not been accepted as evidence of Roman settlement. [Harbison, 1988]

The fort itself is beside an excellent, sheltered harbour and is an ideal landing place for merchants travelling up the Irish Sea. It could have been a native Irish settlement serving as a distribution centre for Roman produce, but it seems far more likely that it was a foreign, perhaps Romano-British, establishment. The closely spaced ditches hint at British or north-west French traditions of fortification, so it could be that the occupants of Drumanagh were an intrusive grouping. [Raftery] In this regard, one translation of the name as 'the Hill of the Menapii' is tantalising because the northern European tribe is listed on Ptolemy's map. It should also be remembered that a settlement of presumed northern British immigrants existed in the 1st century on the island of Lambay, opposite Drumanagh. The material recovered indicates an overwhelming Roman presence on the promontory in the early centuries AD. The matter for debate is the precise nature of this presence. The question of whether the dominant element at Drumanagh was intrusive Roman, Romano-British or Irish remains to be established.

EARLY MEDIEVAL IRELAND 500-1167

Ireland in the early medieval period probably had a population of less than 500,000. After plagues in the 540s and the 660s to 680s, this may have decreased slightly by the time the Vikings arrived. What is known is that around the time of St. Patrick's mission to Ireland, agricultural techniques began to improve,

Early medieval grave slabs at Clonmacnoise, Co. Offaly, a monastery founded in the 6th century by St Ciaran.

with a corresponding decrease in forest cover as more land was brought into production. By the 7th century, when records really begin, laws about land, trespass, fencing and the rights and obligations of landowners appear in the manuscripts. It is from this period that the majority of the 45,000 identified ring-forts emerge as the habitus of farming groups, with associated craft-working, primarily related to the functional ironwork necessary for agriculture.

Early Christian Ireland was a period of transformation. By the 7th century, it was producing high-quality metalwork, manuscripts and literature, without anything in the preceding centuries suggesting that this lay ahead. Without doubt, the influence of Romanised Britain came across the Irish Sea and, whether by trade, marriage or settlement, the art of that period, known to us now as 'Celtic Art', began through cultural exchange. The skills and versatility of Romanised Britons fused with remnants of a western Iron Age La Tène tradition, and produced a unique style that would ultimately reach its finest expression through Christian art. [de Paor, 1958]

Whatever the origins of the incomers of the early centuries AD, by around the year 550, it is suggested that the island had stabilised into two separate 'overlordships'. These were the Uí Neill, who claimed the northern half of the country from their base at Tara, and the Eoganacht, whose territorial power was southerly and centred at Cashel. The inhabitants of Leinster disputed with the Uí Neill the rights to the kingship of Tara and this, according to the annals, was the cause of ongoing warfare.

The annals themselves were part mythology, part genealogy and part dynastic propaganda. The context of their writing is really unknown and the truth of their contents is open to question. However, they do give a sense of early Irish society, and their literary style was the beginning of a tradition that continued into the 17th century with such distinguished writers as Keating, O'Flaherty and MacFirbhisigh.

The massive castle of Kanturk was built by Dermod MacOwen MacDonough around 1600 with gardens, panelled rooms and many Renaissance architectural features. After the Battle of Kinsale and the collapse of Gaelic Ireland, he was instructed by the English Privy Council to halt the building work and tradition suggests it was never completed.

By around 800, the north of the island had the Ulaidh east of the river Bann, the Airgialla in south-central Ulster and the Northern Uí Neill in the area where Donegal, Sligo and part of Coleraine are today. West of the Shannon where Mayo and Galway are now was dominated by the Connachta and the Southern Ui Neill controlled the mid-lands from the Shannon to the east coast. Leinster was the tribal homeland of the Laigin and the south of the island was known as Mumu under the Eoganacht. If we accept the prehistorical nature of the early annals, the island was historically divided into five provincial kingdoms. Border conflict was the theme of the greatest of the ancient sagas, although mythology is not a reliable guide to anything except the exotic imagination of the teller and reader.

GAELIC LIFE

In Ireland, possibly because of incessant feuding, Gaelic families of the early Middle Ages were slow to adopt the administrative staff deemed so essential to an English noble household. There are few, if any, records for notable Gaelic families of the Middle Ages, and only isolated references to officers of state...those who would have managed the land, mortgages, rents, payments and so on. Local officials existed for the collection of rents and payments in kind, and the Knight of Kerry was the hereditary collector of the rents in Kerry for the Earl of Desmond, receiving five per cent for his work.

Irish judges and lawyers were, like other professional groups, mainly hereditary. The most important of these were the Mac Egans and the Mac Clancys. The McGilligans of Magilligan in Ulster were probably hereditary Brehons to the O'Dohertys since they occupied Termon Land, usually assigned to professional jurists, and Donough McGilligan is named in the state papers as 'liaising between Sir Niall Garve O'Donnell and Sir Cahir O'Doherty during the revolt of the latter'. [1641] In the North, Brehon judges such as Art Mac Cawell who was 'Judge to the O'Neill', were usually drawn from these ecclesiastical lawyers. In addition to their fees for every case, the Brehons were also entitled to a retainer from the territory in which they exercised their jurisdiction. In 16th-century Kilkenny, the Brehons were entitled to a pig every second year from every townland. The Brehons were also important witnesses to contracts and some peculiar customs, whereby oaths were sworn on the hand of the local lord. In Kerry, James, Earl of Desmond took land from a kinsman who had falsely sworn that he had not stolen hawks from a neighbour. To break an oath sworn on the hand of an O'Neill incurred a fine 'as the bishops and the best learned in the country shall adjudge, sometimes 60 kine [cattle], other times more.' [Nicholls, 1973]

Christianity and Ireland

RELAND BEFORE CHRISTIANITY was probably culturally similar to Gaul of the last centuries BC in that the people spoke a Celtic language and had ancient traditions, usually centred on the sacred person of the king. As an individual, he embodied the qualities of judge, king and general and was descended from a divine ancestor. His inauguration and role incorporated rites and taboos from the earliest known civilisations of the Indo-Europeans. Very little is known about Ireland in the centuries preceding Christianity, but around the time that St. Patrick appeared, changes began in the landscape that would alter the forest cover and begin the great cattle economy that lasted into the modern period.

In broad terms, Christianity in Ireland reached a missionary peak around the year 500. As a religion, it was much simpler than paganism and had a progressive social message with a strong ethical content. It was well organised through its connection with the Roman Empire, which in the early years had usefully produced plenty of martyrs, whose numerous remains were subdivided to provide relics. The first Christian state was Armenia in 303, followed by the Empire itself in 337. Dissent was a feature from early on and various doctrines competed. Was God the Father separate from God the Son? Was Christ completely divine or were the human and divine bits separate?

There was a struggle between these viewpoints as different 'Christianities' developed in response to local patriotic needs. In Britannia and Hibernia, Pelagianism was the favourite, and its emphasis on this life rather than the next seemed to strike a chord in the character of the people of the two islands. [McEvedy, 1983]

To most scholars, medieval Ireland begins around the 5th century arrival of St. Patrick, a Roman Briton who returned to Ireland to preach and convert the Irish. His mission is traceable only through his own writings and he was not the first Christian on the island as St. Declan of Ardmore and Palladius were certainly in Ireland by AD 430. St. Patrick was, however, successful in a heroic fashion, in that is remembered as the national saint who established Christianity. In general, the Church was the great civilising influence of early medieval Europe, and Patrick's mission in Ireland coincides with the beginnings of Christianity's European popularity. The Roman Empire under Constantine had been nominally Christian since AD 312, although large parts of Gaul and Britain remained pagan. Britain had Christians since the year AD 207 and had organised dioceses by the 4th century, when British bishops attended a conference in Arles in Provence in the year 318. [Ó'Cróinín, 1995] Christianity was not a popular religion in Britannia, and the Romano-Britons continued to prefer their old pagan gods, such as Nodens, better known to Irish people as Nuada of the Silver Arm.

THE CHURCH

The first Christians in Ireland were probably established through slave and trading links with Roman Britain in the east and south of the country, as evidenced by the papally backed mission of Bishop Palladius to the 'Irish believing in Christ' in 431. Their early churches still remain in place-names such as Dunshaughlin (Domnach Sechnaill, the Church of Secundius) and Kilashee (Cell Ausaile, the Church of Auxilius), both in Leinster.

The early Celtic church took its early inspiration from the training

The monastic High-Cross of Castledermot, Co. Kildare, founded in the 9th century and plundered by the Vikings in 1048.

its monks received from St. Ninian at Whithorn in modern Scotland and the monastery of St. David at Menavia in Wales. The ability of the Irish monks to master Latin composition and biblical exegesis was exceptional and by the 8th century the Irish church was respected, powerful and wealthy.

Having enjoyed a remarkable period of cultural and spiritual life, the early church had probably passed its peak when the Vikings began their attacks in the 8th century. While undoubtedly still attracting those of a genuine vocation, it had succumbed to the temptations of secularism, in a similar way to the church elsewhere. The Irish clergy was increasingly drawn from the noble Gaelic

High-Cross from Clonmacnoise, Co. Offaly, founded in the 6th century by St. Ciaran families, and their benefices or livings were passed on from father to son. This right of succession was recognised by the Brehon Laws which stated, *'The tribe of the patron saint shall succeed to the church as long as there shall be a person fit to be an abbot of the said tribe of the patron saint, even though there should be but a psalm singer of them, it is he that will obtain the abbacy.'* St. Colmcille of Iona was succeeded by his first cousin and the third to the fifth, seventh to ninth and eleventh to thirteenth abbots were drawn from the same family. [de Breffny, 1976]

A reform movement, known as the Ceili De, was a reaction to church decadence, and Finglas and Tallaght were both monasteries with strong connections to this movement. The Vikings began their attacks on the monasteries in 795, although from 841 they established settlements at Dublin and other coastal sites. By 1035 there was a Norse bishop of Dublin. But the years following the first Viking attack were nevertheless a widespread, if infrequent, record of attack and pillage, often by Irish chieftains who had discovered that threatened divine retribution was certainly not in this world.

The 12th-century arrival of the Normans began an ecclesiastical reform movement that reinvigorated the existing monasteries and laid out the diocesan boundaries, corresponding to various tribal territories. Led by Malachy of Armagh, Augustinians and Cistercians were brought to Ireland and the Normans introduced Knights Hospitallers who tended the sick and those suffering from incurable diseases. Although the Black Death of 1348/49 had a serious effect on these communities, by the end of the 14th century there were over 500 monasteries and friaries in the country, 90 convents and over 200 hospitals and hospices. Together with some 35 secular colleges founded mainly in the 13th century, the church was community centre, social services and education provider. [Dudley Edwards, 1973]

GRAIGUENAMANAGH

Duiske (or Graiguenamanagh) is one of the best examples of a successful religious foundation. The Cistercian monks of Vallis Sancti

Salvatoris in Stanley, Wiltshire went there in 1207 to found the monastery. They were invited by William Marshall, Lord of Leister and tried several locations before settling along the Dubh Uisce river, from where the monastery takes its Latin name, Duiske. It is the largest Cistercian church in Ireland and its plan is identical to Strata Florida, an abbey in Cardiganshire. Its nave of seven bays, three chapels and a tower shelter beautiful windows and a processional doorway with exceptional carvings, probably by the same masons who worked on Kilkenny Cathedral. The monks here became incredibly successful as wool merchants, having agents in Dublin and Waterford selling their produce to European buyers. [Duignan, 1964]

In the Eastern Catholic Church, a doctrine of homage to the Virgin Mary developed through Cyril of Alexandria. It became formalised at the Council of Ephesus in 431, but it was another three hundred years before it began to flower, principally in Byzantium (now Istanbul) in the 8th century. Three theologians developed the doctrine: Andrew of Crete, John of Damascus and Germanus of Constantinople. What became the Greek Orthodox Church was the source for the Marian hymn *Akathistos* and the prayer beginning Sub Tuum, 'We fly to thy patronage'. Several churches became centres of Marian devotion, and the Emperor Charles the Bald presented the tunic she wore at the annunciation to the monks at Chartres in France in 896. The relic worked miracles and by 1144 a church was being built. After a fire, they built bigger and better. This time, one of the world's greatest structures, financed by France's richest diocese, rose as the Cathedral of Nôtre Dame de Chartres. The materials for this immense structure were carried by rich and poor alike, united in a faith that symbolised the civilising of the barbarian mind through the forgiving of enemies and the seeking of divine forgiveness for one's own transgressions. But Chartres, perhaps for the first time in western art at least, takes the use of stained-glass as a sensual blur of colour into another realm of experience. Having visited the cathedral, my feeling is that the multiplicity of deeply saturated colour images instructed the faithful, yes, but also enthraled the senses.

The Cloister Garth at the Franciscan abbey, Quin, Co. Clare, rebuilt around 1433 by Sioda Cam Macnamara.

But from the point of view of a secular 21st century, deeply felt religious belief, while still being a recent phenomenon in Ireland, has largely disappeared as a majority event in the English-speaking world. In the Middle Ages, the majority of people in Ireland were very religious, like their European contemporaries, but one of the differences between Ireland and the rest of Christendom is that Irish Christianity remained religious, never achieving the level of secular power that it had elsewhere. Except for a small number of individuals, it never became the powerful social system that it was in France, and its bishops did not rule anything more than their congregations.

CLERICAL MARRIAGE

While clerical marriage was forbidden in theory, it was quite common in practice. The most striking feature of Irish clerical positions in medieval Ireland was its hereditary nature and, as mentioned earlier, efforts to enforce celibacy came to nothing. Europe was similar, in that a distinguished career in the church was a normal career for men of noble birth. For centuries, the diocese of Killala was the undisputed property and sinecure of the Ó Maoilfhaghmhair family, while even smaller parish churches were passing from priest to son, by the year 1200.

The accession of Pope John XXII in 1316 encouraged hereditary clerical families with the introduction of dispensations, a way of raising money for the twin papacy that existed at that time. John O'Grady, Archbishop of Cashel from 1332 to 1345 was father of another John O'Grady who became Archbishop of Tuam in 1365, who in turn fathered a third John, succeeding as Bishop of Elphin. The O'Gradys eventually ran out of bishops and Nicholas, the son of John, Bishop of Elphin, could manage only to be the Abbot of Tuamgraney, Chief of his name and father of the Canon of Killaloe.

The 14th-century Bishop Maurice O'Kelly of Clonfert was married and three of his sons entered the Church, one following his father as Bishop of Clonfert and the other as Bishop of Tuam. The most pious of the three entered the Cistercians at Knockmoy, becoming abbot and fathering two sons, one of whom became rector of Athenry and the other, Archdeacon of Clonfert. The famous Annals of Ulster were collected and written by a cleric whose fourteen children were calmly entered into the record like the sons of other gentry and notables. [Nicholls, 1973]

THE PAPACY

In Europe, the Papacy was as important as any emperor, although its nepotism was curtailed after a convocation of cardinals, established on the instructions of Gregory IX, became the electoral body charged with choosing a Pope. Amazingly for the time, majority decision was introduced, to avert the 'two pope' problem that had existed between 1059 and 1179, when no effective method had been devised for making a decision. At that time, the Roman nobility, led by a faction known as the 'Tusculiani', elected John, Cardinal-Bishop of Velettri as Benedict X. He was rejected by supporters of the late Pope Stephen IX and eventually a council degraded his status and he was deposed. The 'new' notion of a two-thirds' majority conclave was revolutionary, removing both the mysterious divine choice element and the reality of political chicanery from Papal succession. A 'Great Schism' occurred from 1378 to 1415 and before it ended there were three Popes, three colleges of cardinals, and Christendom was in chaos and confusion.

By the beginning of the 15th century, Irish church reformers were attempting to oust the families from their traditional sees and benefices. Provincial synods in Armagh (1426) and Cashel (1453) legislated in canon law against clerical marriage, threatening excommunication and deprivation of the sacraments for those who refused to 'put away' their wives and concubines. A famous case taken by the grandson of a bishop, Laurence O'Gallagher, himself Bishop of Raphoe from 1442 to 1478, was to request that he retain his seat and obtain preferment for his seven sons. The case was successful,

despite canon laws to the contrary. He was denounced for fornication in 1469 and suspended, but obtained absolution from a court in Rome through a succession of Irish intermediaries, who were 'persuaded' by the medieval equivalent of a stuffed brown envelope.

The clergy were occasionally involved in small wars between different families, who were often related as well. Bishop O'Connell of Killala was driven from his see by the O'Dowdas, who installed an O'Dowda in his place. The other local dynasty, the Barretts, supported O'Connell, and fighting broke out, with killings on both sides. A mini war occurred in Cork in 1474 between William Roche and Gerald FitzGerald over who would succeed to the diocese of Cloyne and Ross. FitzGerald won, so William Roche and his sons brought their private army and, in revenge, sacked and burned the town of Cloyne.

Violent Change

4

S IGNS AND PORTENTS were still indicators of things to come to the man and woman of the early Middle Ages. And as the 8th century wound on, eclipses of the sun and moon were recorded as being of special significance, while dragons were seen in the air. In the Christian understanding of things, the world might have been coming to an end. The portents returned in 767 and 788 when great thunder and lightning began a 'terrible fit of panic fear' called *Lamhchomart* or the clapping of hands. The response of the clergy to these strange happenings was to call for two fasts, together with fervent prayer, that the country might be delivered until Michaelmas. Perhaps their fervent offerings worked for a while at least. The first Danish raid took place in 795, when Rathlin Island, off the Antrim coast, was plundered and the houses burnt. The raiders originated mainly in Denmark and Norway (Danes and Norse) and were also distinguished as Finn Galls, 'Fair Foreigners', possibly from their light hair colour, and Dubh Galls, 'Black Foreigners', possibly of a dusky hue from Jutland. For almost two centuries these pirates terrorised England and Ireland and were characterised as being ruthless, cruel and without mercy. They attacked the monastery of Bangor in 888 and killed over 700 people, including the abbot and the monks.

The northern coastal settlements were harassed and plundered for almost 20 years until the attackers were defeated by the northern kings and their armies in 811 and 825, their northern power being finally destroyed by the Uí Neill in 866. The damage caused by the Vikings and subsequent Irish copycat-raiders left the monasteries bereft of scriptoria, as capable monks fled to Europe, taking both manuscripts and the skill of illumination with them.

The word 'Viking' is Old Norse for Sea Robber, and was applied to those mobile groups who lurked in the vik or inlets of western Norway, waiting to pounce on passing ships. In general they were the younger sons of farmers and petty kings, with little likelihood of any inheritance. Initially their raids were sporadic hit-and-run affairs and the first 25 years of Viking contact records 26 attacks on Irish settlements by Norse, compared to 87 by the Irish. It appears that plundering and burning of monasteries was well established before the Viking wars. In general terms, the Irish monasteries were tempting to Viking and Irish raider alike for the treasures within. Almost every church at this time would have contained small silver or enamelled caskets for holding relics, and many were the treasuries for the local kings. They were the principal economic centres of Ireland, with land, livestock and the related wealth from trade.

VIKING TOWNS

In the North Sea, the demise of the Frisians in northern Germany left a power vacuum which was exploited by Danish and Norwegian Vikings. Their skill in seamanship and navigation meant their over-population difficulties could be sent somewhere else. By the mid-9th century, fleets of Viking ships were on the Boyne and the Liffey and their army defeated the Irish under Uí Neill. They began an attempt to conquer England, and Norsemen overran the Shetland and Hebridean islands while Danes attacked the centre of England. Kenneth MacAlpin united the Picts and Scots, as the Irish of what became Scotland were called, and by 878 the Danes had been defeated by Alfred, King of the Anglo-Saxons. By 918, the Danes of England were forced to recognise the kings of Wessex (most of southern England). Elsewhere, Danish Vikings succeeded in establishing themselves in northern France and in 911, Normandy was established as their duchy.

Viking settlement in inland Leinster was mainly of a trading nature, based around monasteries such as Clondalkin near Dublin and St. Mullins, on the Barrow. There is some evidence of other settlements at Rath Torcaill, near Blessington, and Lyons in north Kildare. The remains from these sites are small and only one has produced the 'hogback' type of reclining gravestone found at similar sites in Danish-controlled England. The Vikings in Ireland seemed content to remain traders, and farming does not seem to have been a primary Norse activity. They were a sea-faring, trading people, whose focus was generally seaward. [Clinton, 2000]

Irish trade in that early period was the preserve of the Scandinavians, who traded hides, slaves and furs to Bristol, La Rochelle, Rouen and Bordeaux, bringing back manufactured items unavailable in Ireland. The inhabitants of Viking towns existed independently of their Gaelic hinterland, although paying rents to the kings and frequently marrying into those local dynasties. Many Vikings chose to establish themselves in Ireland and their towns of Dublin, Waterford, Cork and Limerick became Ireland's trading outlets and ports.

NORMAN INTEREST

Ireland had been a temporary refuge for exiled Anglo-Saxons such as Harold, the sons of Harold, and Arnulf of Montgomery. King William Rufus, remembered for his greed and violent temper, apparently considered 'building a bridge of ships' to conquer the land, but it was his successor, King Henry II, who became intimately involved, because Ireland's abundant and fertile land seemed available to the Norman eye. Henry considered Ireland for possible conquest in the 1150s but decided against any involvement.

Kilconell Friary, Co Galway, founded by William O'Kelly, Lord of Hi Many in 1353 on the site of an earlier monastery

During this period Ireland had extensive trading links with England but was regarded in in clerical terms as being subordinate to Canterbury. Lanfranc, Archbishop from 1070 onwards, wanted to establish Canterbury as a primacy such as Milan or Toledo, with jurisdiction over Ireland, England and Scotland

and, although Rome refused, he claimed it anyway.

At the point where Irish and Norman meet is really where civilisations clash. The Irish, having experienced a Christian golden age, seemed to hover, as if enjoying the reflected light from their previous achievements. The Norman was different. It was not a culturally deep ethos, but it was ambitious and progressive, however brutal it appears from our perspective. Ireland's physical distance had allowed a cultural depth and quality to develop unhindered by barbarian invasion and its scholars returned to Europe as missionaries of depth and intelligence. But the church at home suffered. Few intellectuals rose to replace those abroad and the Viking raids served to weaken what was left. St. Bernard, in his life of St. Malachy, describes a church where the elementary duties are well respected, but the clergy are becoming untutored and unlearned. The church in Ireland never rose to being the social force it was becoming in Europe. The Irish church in the 12th century was still monastic, ascetic and spiritual, not temporal.

During the 12th century, however, three synods at Cashel, Rath Breasil and Kells established an independent Irish church, with Armagh at its head. This deliberate movement out of Canterbury's influence meant a loss of income and prestige to the English church and the English bishops sent John of Salisbury to the Pope appealing for his authority and help to bring the Irish Church into submission. With this in mind, Pope Adrian IV issued the bull Laudabiliter, giving Henry II of England the right to rule Ireland and bring the church under Canterbury again. Tradition suggests he sent Henry an emerald ring as a token of their agreement, perhaps creating the popular description of Ireland as 'The Emerald Isle'.

12TH-CENTURY IRISH POLITICS

By 1100, there was no one strong enough to claim the high-kingship of Ireland. Murtagh O'Brien, grandson of the late victorious BrianBorú, was king of a weak and ineffective Munster, left in such a state by the

Pyrrhic victory of Clontarf. While O'Brien was powerful in Munster, he had inadvertently helped the O'Conors of Connacht to power by humbling their rivals, the O'Rourkes of Breffni. O'Brien was known in England, and Arnulf of Montgomery, a powerful Anglo-Welsh magnate who was conspiring against Henry I of England, sought and obtained the hand of one of his daughters. O'Brien also received the mysterious gift of a 'camel' from the King of Alba, although the nature of the beast and the identity of the donor are unclear. Murtagh's father, Turlough O'Brien, was a correspondent with Pope Gregory VII, also writing several times to Anselm of Canterbury, who in 1096 had ordained Mael Isu O'Hanvery as the first bishop of the Hiberno-Scandinavians of Waterford. Murtagh also used the fleet of the Ostmen, as Vikings became known by the 11th century, from Limerick to demonstrate his mastery of the Shannon and, if necessary, the western coast. [Dolley, 1972]

The key to understanding the politics of 12th-century Ireland is the position of Leinster, the kingdom that suffered most from the defeat at Clontarf. It was a region that had several Norse townships that brought the outside world to Leinster and its king, Dermot Mac Mael na Mbo, was more aware than other Irish kings that there was an outside world.

In the summer of 1166, Rory O'Conor, the new High King, convened a great synod of the Gaelic aristocracy at Thlaghta, near Athboy, County Meath. At this meeting were: O'Rourke, King of Breffni; Dunchad O'Carroll, King of Oriel; Eochaid, King of Ulaidh; Ó'Melachlainn, King of Tara; Asgaill Mac Torquil, King of Dublin and many others. They were meeting to divide Ireland between the royal families to restore the political structure of the island after an affray that had led to the death of Muirchertach MacLochlainn, the High King. Conspicuous by his absence was Dermot MacMurrough, King of Leinster, hereditary prince of the Uí Cinnsellaigh, a tribal grouping whose territory comprised the modern diocese of Ferns. Through several years of fighting and diplomacy, Dermot was recognised as King of (south) Leinster and was envious of the northern territories nominally within his jurisdiction. Meath, at the limit of MacMurrough's influence, met the historic territory of Breffni, corresponding to today's Leitrim and Cavan, and was ruled by Tighernan O'Rourke, a bitter rival of Dermot for the land of north Meath.

In 1152, MacMurchada carried off O'Rourke's wife, Dervogilla, apparently without much resistance, but she returned to O'Rourke the following year. For the next 14 years the two princes were opponents in Leinster's wars until O'Rourke enlisted the new King of Connacht, leading to the defeat of MacMurrough's army. Dermot found few friends to defend his kingdom against the (still) cuckolded O'Rourke. His kingdom seemed lost.

In August 1166, Dermot MacMurrough fled to England looking for his friend Henry II who was then in France. He stayed with the Augustinians in Bristol and arranged a formal meeting with the king through an intermediary, Robert FitzHarding. Dermot travelled to Notre Dame de Fontrevaux and met Henry, described as having grey eyes and short reddish hair. Henry was occupied with the war in France and was unwilling to become personally involved, but granted Dermot a licence to recruit from the disaffected Normans in South Wales. He probably had in mind straightforward mercenary soldiers who would return to Wales after their work was finished, and it does not seem likely that he was planning a conquest.

Henry's income up to the 1150s was around £20,000 sterling per annum, compounded of the old danegeld or extortion paid to the Danes of Canute's time and amounts levied when war was at hand. Nigel of Ely, the first treasurer, reorganised the finances in 1159, and his son confirmed the habit of careful finance, so that Henry raised an additional £8,000 per annum by 1168 and was in a position to grant Dermot a large sum to pay for the mercenaries he wished to recruit. [Davis, 1945]

With this money, Dermot tried to interest groups around Bristol for his expedition but to no avail, until he was introduced to a man 'with a face of delicacy, almost feminine, his bearing modest and

reserved, his voice weak and thin, his conversation unassuming.' It was Richard FitzGilbert de Clare, known by his father's nickname, Strongbow. The two men conferred and terms, including the hand of Aoife in marriage and the subsequent inheritance of Leinster, were agreed. Dermot was not in a position to make any such arrangement, having two legitimate sons and a capable illegitimate son, Donal Kavanagh, who was administering his affairs while he was away.

Cahir Castle, Co. Tipperary, rebuilt c. 1375 by James Butler, Earl of Ormond.

Dermot was however following precedent in this arrangement, in that Irish kings had often preferred more able successors than the nearest family member, although Dermot did have a capable illegitimate son, Donal Kavanagh, who ran his affairs while he was away. De Clare, however, was not in a hurry and postponed any adventure while he visited Henry in France. Dermot went to South Wales and had a fruitful meeting with Rhys ap Gruffydd, a Welsh prince with a plethora of Norman-Welsh relations who were becoming a nuisance and available for hire. Dermot came to terms with the Normans and agreed that they would receive the town of Wexford and two adjacent cantreds in return for him recovering Leinster. [Dolley, 1972]

In August 1167, MacMurrough landed at Glascarraig, 12 miles south of Arklow, with more than 400 Norman mercenaries, including Richard FitzGodbert de Roche, an ancestor of the Roches of Munster, and some Flemish archers and managed to recover an area similar to the modern County Wexford. He also paid the huge sum of 100 ounces of gold to O'Rourke in compensation for taking his wife as a mistress.

He spent the following year sulking, having been chastised by the High King, Rory O'Conor. He sent his chancellor, O'Regan, to South Wales that autumn with the poetic message [as reported by Giraldus Cambrensis]

We have watched the stork and the swallow;
The birds of summer have come and gone;

*But neither the east wind nor the west has brought us the man we
   wish to see;*
All Leinster is returned to us.
Come with speed and with a strong hand;
Then shall the four provinces bow down before the fifth.

[DAVIS, 1937]

On 1 May 1169, they obliged. Three ships anchored in Bannow Bay
with 90 armoured knights and 300 Welsh archers, whose weapon, the
Longbow, could send an arrow through two inch-oak planking and
the strongest armour. Further ships arrived the following day with
more archers and knights, and Dermot and his elder son Donal
joined them with a force of 500 Leinstermen. Having taken the town
of Wexford, Dermot and his allies then fought MacGillapatrick, who
had blinded Dermot's younger son, Eanna, the previous year.

There follows in this part of Irish history the usual changing of
sides, secret deals, ambushes, broken promises, Norman vs.
Norman, Irish vs. Irish and, ultimately, the intervention of significant
individuals who were prepared to commit greater resources for a
greater return.

In August 1170, another 200 armoured knights and 1,000 men-at-
arms and archers arrived at Bannow Bay. There was now a serious
army on Irish soil, far more professional and committed than anything at the call of an Irish king. Strongbow had borrowed heavily
from the moneylenders of Gloucestershire to finance the expedition
and the main payment for his hired men was the promise of land.

At the end of 1170, however, Strongbow was in a weak position.
On paper, he was the heir of Dermot MacMurrough, but there were
others more likely to be supported by the MacMurroughs and their
allies. His king, Henry II, was aware of the possibility of a Norman
kingdom in Ireland and demanded his return while the hibernicised
Vikings, the 'Ostmen', were determined to resist the new overlords
by the use of their Dublin fleet, able to intercept any Normans cross-
ing from Pembrokeshire. Strongbow and Dermot marched to

Dublin and outmanoeuvred Rory O'Conor's army camped at Clondalkin. The Ostmen of Dublin, crestfallen at Rory's mistake, offered to surrender on terms. Strongbow began discussions with the Archbishop of Dublin, Laurence O'Toole, but his men broke the truce and the Normans poured into the city intent on plunder. Hasculf, the Jarl (Scandinavian Earl) of Dublin and most of the Norse escaped on already laden boats and went to the Isle of Man, where they remained.

The 12th-century Norman Motte at Nobber, Co. Meath, guarding the ford on the river Dee. Mottes were the first fortifications of the Normans and are found in almost every Eastern county.

Early in 1171, MacMurrough went into mourning following assassinations within the Irish camp and the killing of hostages, who included Dermot's son, Conor, and a son of Donal Kavanagh by the High King, Rory O'Conor. The Normans attempted to stave off Henry's demands that they return to Wales by Easter 1171 or face forfeiture of their lands. Strongbow went to his overlord at Newenham and found that Henry had decided upon an Irish expedition, with the intent of adding the country to his possessions. He pardoned Strongbow for the invasion, taking the seaports as his own and allowing the Earl to return quietly to his still considerable possessions in Ireland.

Eventually, in October, Henry arrived in person with 500 armoured knights and 3,500 men-at-arms, complete with a siege train, in case any town should be foolish enough to resist. To the Irish, they were now in a different and more threatening situation. These were not the amateur soldiers of kings and high kings, but a Panzer Division against whom the Irish had little strategy and inferior weapons.

On the spiritual side, the Irish bishops accepted the liturgical uniformity that he sought to introduce, each of them sending him official recognition, under their individual personal seal. Through this act, he was accepted by them as the rightful overlord of Ireland in accordance with Laudabiliter, the papal decree that Henry had invoked. Archbishop Donal O'Houlihan of Cashel met the King and a reforming synod was agreed. Henry hoped this would reassure Rome that he was a dutiful son of the Church. As Henry continued his progress around Ireland, the MacCarthys, O'Mahonys, O'Briens and other kings did homage. However the High King, Rory O'Conor, sulking behind the Shannon, appeared unable to comprehend the events that were to change his position and that of every king from then on.

Following Henry's triumphal tour, papal letters arrived from Alexander III congratulating the Irish hierarchy on the reorganisation of its Church and praising the Irish princes who had accepted Henry as overlord. The Irish kings believed they were obtaining guarantees against Norman land-grabbing and Henry thought he was being generous with his own land. But he made a huge grant to Hugh de Lacy, who was presented with the entire territory of Meath, stretching from the east coast to the Shannon at Athlone. This huge area had, of course, to be forcibly taken from those whose land it was. DeLacy was the first justiciar or chief governor and also commander of the Dublin garrison. [Davis, 1945]

In 1175, however, Rory O'Conor and Henry agreed to a private treaty that allowed Rory to keep most of Connacht,

The black limestone tomb of Margaret FitzGerald, Countess of Ormond, who died in 1542 and was interred in St. Canices Cathedral.

The rich lands of Meath, covering over 1,000 square miles, granted by King Henry to Hugh de Lacy in the 12th century.

acknowledge Henry and his successors, and pay up one in ten of every cattle hide in Ireland. If similar binding treaties had been proposed and adhered to, Ireland might have become an Anglo-Irish country, blending Celt and Norman, since Henry seemed intent, initially at least, to offer justice to all, provided they recognised his suzerainty.

As soon as Henry left the country, the Normans began work in earnest and murdered Donal O'Farrell of Longford, Murrough MacMurrough of Leinster and Tighernan O'Rourke of Breffni, whose mutilated head and body were displayed on the gates of Dublin. The Normans had borrowed heavily from moneylenders and knew that the rate of interest charged, if unpaid, would soon outstrip the capital borrowed. They were under pressure to obtain land by any means, resell what they did not want and farm the rest for cash crops.

In addition, Henry retrospectively granted *all* of Ulster to John de Courcy in 1176 because de Courcy had gained control of most of the province, although Cambrensis claims that, as a lord, he maintained good peace with all his subjects without distinction of race. Henry, however, decided that Ireland should be the personal fiefdom of his favourite son John, whom history portrays as a dissolute waster. When he arrived in 1185, John angered the Normans, insulted the Irish and spent the money his father had given him on endless partying with his friends.

By the start of the 13th century, Ireland and Wales were enduring a similar relationship with England in that different customs, traditions and language met in a political arena removed from a central core of power. However, Ireland, more than its Welsh neighbour, was a world of interlocking and competing families in that period, using English law when it suited and Irish when it didn't.

Within a few centuries, the Norman invasion and intended conquest of Ireland was over, probably due to several factors, the most important being the political collapse of England. Royal authority had shrunk to an area within a day's ride of Dublin Castle and no more. It existed within certain towns, but this was a usual arrangement in the Middle Ages, where king and town had a common interest in resisting the encroachments of the nobility and their fondness for taxes and exactments.

English Ireland by the 14th century had become a network of lineages and families. Government control could be effective only through the co-operation and cajolement of these families. Like Gaelic Ireland, English Ireland family and kinship ties were not always confined to a specific area. With relatives, sons, daughters and cousins scattered across the island, allegiances were divided through geography and community. Identity was maintained by the more dominant families, who, while feuding internally on an intermittent basis, could recombine when faced with an external threat. The descendants of the Normans were conscious of the ancestry as much as the Gaelic nobility and when Edmund Butler (d.1321) granted a moiety to his favourite church in Gowran, Co. Kilkenny in return for a daily Mass, the priests had to pray for some 11 generations by name. [Frame, 1982]

13TH CENTURY

The first Great Council to be called a Parliament was held in England in 1258 and the first Irish Parliament (excluding a 'commons') met at Castledermot, Co. Kildare in 1264, attended by Irish clergy and lords of the Anglo-Norman nobility. The higher clergy were part of most of the parliaments of medieval Ireland, frequently acting as go-betweens for their Gaelic lords, but it was not until the reign of Henry VIII that Gaelic nobles were able to attend.

A political precedent was set in 1224 when Cathal Croibhdhearg O' Conor wrote to Henry III of England stating that he was prepared to waive the infringements of the Normans in Connacht in return for security of the lands he still held. The same security was not available to other Irish lords, owing to the ongoing attempts of the Normans to seize the better and richer lands.

Since Henry was only 16 years old at the time, the government of England was in the hands of Hubert de Burgh, who was also justiciar, or Chief Justice. It was probably he who petitioned for the new grant of land in Connacht to be made to Richard de Burgo. Henry III was not a particularly strong king politically although he had a developed aesthetic sense, fully realised in the great abbey he commissioned for Westminster. He was caught between groups of powerful nobles attempting to gain access to power through his patronage. They succeeded in forcing him to agree to a council whereby they would make up 50 per cent of the number, to balance the French appointees favoured by his father. It appears that he began granting land in Ireland to the de Burgos to gain support in England. In 1250, Henry III tried his hand at a crusade, borrowing a fortune from the Pope, but the cash was diverted into a scheme to create a mini kingdom of Sicily for his second son, Edmund. The scheme failed, the crusade collapsed and Henry owed the Pope a fortune.

ULSTER

There was a moment in the 13th century that suggested the begin-

nings of a national sentiment. It came at the end of a series of intrusions by the Justiciar or chief governor attempting to subdue Ulster. In 1241, Maelseachlainn Ó'Domhnaill became King of Tir Conaill and, with his help, Brian O'Neill became King of Tir Eoghain, defeating in battle the last of the MacLochlainn line, who were favourable to the Viceroy and acknowledged the dominion of de Courcy, Earl of Ulster. The Justiciar of that

The keep of Donegal Castle, erected in the 15th century by the O'Donnells and home to Ineen Dubh, one of the most formidable women in medieval politics.

time was Maurice FitzGerald, a descendant of the original Normans; he was determined to complete the conquest of Ulster and Connacht. He succeeded in Connacht and the O'Conors became his ally, retaining the title of king.

In 1247, FitzGerald built a castle at Sligo as a base for operations along the Erne. He moved on Ballyshannon, outmanoeuvred the O'Donnells and killed the King of Tir Conaill and MacSomhairlidh, leader of Hebridean Gallowglass, or hired fighting men. The following year he marched on Coleraine and Beleek, where he built a castle as another step in the plan. Brian O'Neill moved swiftly and, astonishingly, brought a fleet of ships overland from Lough Foyle to Lough Erne and attacked and demolished the castle – an extraordinary feat of logistics and strategy.

In 1257, Godfrey O'Domhnaill, King of Tir Conaill, destroyed the castle at Caoluisce near Beleek and burnt Sligo. He received wounds during that battle from which he was to die later.

But in 1258, an event occurred which suggests a feeling of nationhood or at least the acknowledgement of being different and the right to be so. Tadgh O'Brien, King of Thomond, Aedh O'Conor, King of Connacht, and the nobility of their territories assembled at the shattered castle of Caoluisce near Sligo and met Brian O'Neill, King of Tyrone. According to the annals, they gave their obedience to O'Neill as the supreme authority. In effect, they created a monarchy of Ireland. A side event, O'Neill's unnecessary attack near Letterkenny in Donegal on the dying Godfrey O'Donnell O'Domhnaill did not deter his enthusiasm. The O'Cahan Lords of Inishowen and several Connacht chieftains joined in an attempt to oust these invaders, attacking de Courcy and his knights. They were defeated by the archers and opponents' armour in a violent and bloody clash. Brian and 23 leaders of the Ulster nobility were killed, leaving de Courcy in control of east Ulster. The MacDonlevys never recovered their lands and by 1280 they were to be found in service as physicians with the O'Domhnaill (O'Donnell) of Tir Conaill. Like the O'Clerys of Uí Fiachrach, another 'ex'-royal family, the ancient

MacDuinnsleibhe family, established since at least the 5th century as kings of Dal Fiatach (a portion of east Ulster), was forced to find service and position with other, more powerful monarchies.

In 1259, Aedh O'Connor married the daughter of Dougal Mac Sorley, Lord of the Isles. The dowry included 160 Scotto-Norse mercenaries, the first soldiers in Ireland able to withstand a mounted charge. The Gallowglasses had arrived in Ireland, as revolutionary as the tank in modern warfare. On the way to his wedding, Aedh met Brian O'Neill at Devinish Island and they decided to join forces in an attack on Ulster the following year. By that time, the Anglo-Normans of Ulster were unhappy with being ruled by 'men of English birth' and there was considerable bad feeling amongst the colonists against English interference in Ulster generally. Brian O'Neill could have used this resentment to forge an alliance with de Courcy and the Anglo-Normans and oust the justiciar's feudal army, but instead he attacked the very people who might have supported him. It all came to a sad end at Drumdearg, near Downpatrick on 14 May 1259 when O'Neill, the O'Cahan of Inishowen and the flower of Ulster and Connacht chivalry fell, achieving nothing except militant animosity from the Ulster colonists.

The second result of Aedh's useless attempts at politics was the hatred he had created in the O'Donnells by his needless attack on the dying Godfrey the previous year. The O'Donnells had married into the MacSweeneys, a powerful Gallowglass (see Chapter 6) family and, with their support, were building a dynasty in Donegal which, as a result of Brian's attack, would be antagonistic to the O'Neills for centuries to come. [Dolley, 1972]

ENGLISH POLITICS

By 1275, the Irish were demanding full rights under English law. But the following year Henry III ratified the Treaty of Paris, renouncing his rights to Normandy and Anjou, so his focus was on his remaining French holdings. He retained Gascony, but only as a fief of the king of France. Between 1258 and 1265 there was a political struggle for control of England, with the popes threatening excommunication or promising dispensation as required to support the king. Eventually the barons rose under Simon de Montfort, an adventurer eager to make his fortune and marry well. He secretly married Henry's widowed sister and tried to reform the functions of the monarchy. He was killed on 4 August 1265 at the Battle of Evesham.

14TH CENTURY

From 1307 to 1327, England was ruled by Edward II, whom the nobility hated. He disliked jousting, hunting and hawking and preferred the ordinary activities of his poorer subjects, such as rowing and thatching. England's nobility detested his behaviour, feeling that he was demeaning the status of his royal office, attempting to oust corrupt officials and replace them with Frenchmen instead. Because of poor military leadership and a superior Scots army, the English were thrashed on Midsummer Day 1314 at Bannockburn, establishing Scotland's freedom. Another facet in Edward's character was the particular attention he paid to his 'favourite', Piers Gaviston. It made him a hated man. They were probably lovers, although Edward married Isabella of France and she produced a son and heir. Despite the obvious dangers of disregarding the powerful nobility, Edward continued to give land, titles and money to Gaviston, who was banished by a law passed by the barons. Despite this law, Gaviston returned and flaunted his intimacy with the king. Eventually, he was pursued by the barons to Scarborough Castle where, after a siege, he surrendered and was beheaded. In 1327 Edward was killed also, except that, as king, he could not be killed by anything that left a mark on his body. He was brutally slain in Berkeley Castle it is said, by having a red-hot roasting spit shoved deep into his bowels.

The whole reign of Edward II was probably the weakest era in English medieval history and a time when Ireland, with more foresight, might have achieved the same level of independence as Scotland.

Medieval Life

5

GIRALDUS CAMBRENSIS, although scathing in his social descriptions of Ireland in the 12th century, was complimentary when it came to the music of the country. He compared it to the music of Wales, finding Welsh 'rapid and precipitate' while the Irish sounded 'slow and solemn' but he enjoyed the Irish harpists, whose 'skill in these matters, being incomparably superior to any other nation I have seen.' He was amazed at the 'intricate arrangement of the notes, with melodies so harmonious and perfect' and how the Irish musicians appeared to 'delight in so much delicacy and soothe so softly, that the excellence of their art lieth in concealing what they do.' [Haverty, 1886]

Music and poetry were two important parts of the cultural life of medieval Ireland. As described in the Carew manuscripts, 'Harpers, rhymers, Irish chroniclers, bards ... go praising in rhymes the gentlemen of the Pale ... procuring a talent [liking] of Irish disposition and conversation in them ... which is likewise convenient to be expelled.' The Dublin administration of 1537 recognised that poets, especially, singing the praises of 'Great Men', should not be allowed to travel the country because their songs, 'provoketh the people to an Irish order.'

HOSPITALITY

There were other forms of entertainment and even warriors needed rest and recreation. A poem of the 16th century gives a genteel picture of Irish hospitality and a hostess.

> Graceful hospitality is ministered
> To all who come each night,
> At the quiet banquet of the populous mansion
> By the placid, generous, cheerful dame.
>
> [ANON. *translation from Gaelic, c.1590*]

Irish hospitality seems to have been a tradition since before the 10th century and 'ale, a bath and a large fire' were 'the first thing ye need', according to St. Ciaran. In the monasteries and friaries, the monks enjoyed a varied diet of wild swan, quails and oysters and drank mead, a satisfying blend of wine, honey and cinnamon. Imported wine fron Spain was served in the castles of the rich. Many served 'usquebaugh', a whiskey very popular with 'musicianers', especially harpists and accompanying poets. This drink came under licensing control from 1664. Edmund Spenser, a fine poet himself and a speculator in Irish property, remarked on the sweet wit and good judgement of the Irish poets. Part of their function was to use rhyme and repetition to remind rich and poor alike of their common descent and mutual obligations. Even in medieval Ireland, poets still had a pride of place as their ancestors had done in the days of the High Kings. The farmers and the poor ate 'bonnyclabber, mulahaan and choak-cheese', probably types of curds or yoghurt, but everyone enjoyed local beer. The potato possibly arrived with Walter Raleigh around 1580, and by 1620, boxty bread, a mixture of flour and potatoes, was popular with all classes.

CULTIVATION OF THE LAND

The ownership of land for cattle or cultivation was in the hands of a

Gaelic ruling class whose tenants lived as tenants-at-will, with little or no legal rights to their holdings. They were bound through obligations to that ruling elite and some at least preferred the Norman feudal arrangements, offering some security within the Anglicised lordships that abutted the Gaelic territories. The unit of measurement of agricultural land was the 'ploughland' of 120 acres, excluding 'rivers, water meadows, moors, hylls and wodds.' This allowed around 300 cows per eight ploughlands or around 1,000 acres. In England, the foot was standardised as a measurement in the reign of Henry I (1100-35) and by 1272 the standard acre was reckoned to be 66 feet by 660 feet. The extent of arable land in Munster was measured by the number of days it took to plough. [MacCurtain, 1972]

The monasteries were the exemplar in agricultural practice and

The 15th-century curtain wall of the Augustinian Priory of Kells in County Kilkenny, founded in 1193 and containing in its heyday a hospital, brewhouse, school, church and residence for the Canons. During recent excavations, herbs used in medieval medicine were found growing wild, near where the monks had their kitchen garden and hospital over 600 years ago.

St. Benedict in his *Rule* laid down a balance of intellectual study and physical work. By the 13th century, lay gardeners were working the soil for the Benedictines and the great agricultural estates had become a Cistercian trademark. There was a division between the non-labouring choir monks and the labouring *conversi* or lay-brothers, since the monks were drawn from the Gaelic and Anglo-Norman gentry, and were above manual labour. In Germany, St. Dorothy of the Cherries was a favourite saint of gardeners and St. Fiacre, often shown with a Bible and a spade, was universally popular.

The parts of the human body were a guide to measurement in the Middle Ages and a 'foot' and a step (about 2' 6") was used to gauge planting. A hand-span of eight or nine inches gave a suitable distance for planting leeks and the hand width still measures horses. The making of wattle fences had specific instructions 'to be 12 hands high, three bands of wattle, held by posts, each one foot as far as the big toe apart, and each post to get three blows of a mallet.'

Gardening and the cultivation of plants began with the Arab civilisation that discovered horticulture in Persia. It brought that knowledge to Europe through the Moorish (N.African Arab) invasion of Spain in the early Middle Ages. The Arabs also used Greek medicine and herbs as pharmaceuticals and, as their medical manuscripts were translated into Latin, a more advanced medicine was brought to Europe. Emperor Charlemagne commissioned the *Capitulare de Villis* in 800 as a treatise on what should be grown on the estates of noblemen. This became a guidebook for horticulture across the Continent, spreading into the monasteries and perhaps into Ireland through the educated monks who travelled to and fro in those times. One particular expert in gardening was the Dominican Albertus Magnus, a veteran traveller who closely observed what he saw and wrote in a work called *De Vegetabilibus et Plantis* in 1260.

The evidence suggests that only within the Pale, the anglicised territories around Dublin, was there a systematic three-field system with ditch-banks separating the farms. An act of 1534 stipulates that 'every husbandman having a plough within the English Pale shall set

by the year, twelve ashes on the ditch and boundarys of his farm.' Gradually, the well-known mearing of a stone-lined ditch between ash and thorn became the accepted mearings [boundaries] within the counties of Louth, Meath and Dublin. The main crops within the Pale were oats and barley, with rye grown west of the Shannon. Turnips and clover appeared from the mid-14th century, and barley in Carlow and Wexford. The Irish monasteries were also agricultural estates and the records taken at the time show that they frequently comprised water-mills, salmon weirs, orchards, arable acreage, gardens and pasturelands. When St. Wolstan's was suppressed in 1534 'on the feast of St. Simon and St. Jude', the last prior, Richard Weston, had 'four gardens, four parks and eight orchards.'

Agricultural prices for 1589 show 'a fat pigge, one pound of butter or two gallons of milk, for 1 penny' and a 'fat mutton for 15 shillings and three pence'. Red deer were plentiful in the Irish

A coat-of-arms, possibly of the Preston or Plunkett family in Duleek churchyard, Co. Louth.

The 15th-century ditch of 'The Pale' – built as a semi-continuous perimeter around the English controlled shires from Ardee, Co. Louth to Dalkey, Co. Dublin, to act as a deterrent to cattle-raiding. Ultimately it represented the outer limit of the medieval English administration.

forests and the usual price for 'a skinned deer, 2s and 5d'. Mayo was 'rich in cattle, deer, hawks and honey', according to the historian Camden, but agriculture gathered pace only after the plantations. Horse breeding was beginning by the end of the 16th century, although it was not fully understood until the later 1600s.

EDUCATION

In Ireland, the ancient sagas and legends were first written down in the 8th century and contained epics such as the *Voyage of Bran*, the *Words of Scathach to Cuchulainn* and heroic tales of Ulster princes. The material used was calfskin, with 92 calves being used for the *Book of Ui Maine*. Given that a good scribe might finish a page per day, it would have taken at least two years to transcribe its 736 pages. Bangor, the abbey founded by St. Comgall (died c. 603), was the source of many of these early texts and since the abbot was succeeded by son and grandson, they recorded their noble genealogies as well as the tales. [O'Neill, 1984]

Occasionally the northern manuscripts record obscure battles elsewhere, as when the tribe of Corco Ochae was annihilated in 552 in Limerick and the fact was recorded by St. Mo Lua, one of their number and a pupil of St. Comghall. Mo Lua established a monastery further south in Clonfertmulloe, on land granted by the Loighes (County Laois) and, in thanks for the land, his monks wrote a glowing pedigree for this subject tribe, showing them to be descended from the legendary Ulster hero, Conall Cernach.

In the medieval period, learned families, which previously had had close relationships with the old Celtic church, became hereditary lawyers, physicians and historians. Together with the many 'hereditary' monks and abbots, they formed an educated and cultivated 'middle-class' based around the monasteries and their associated commercial life. As the monasteries grew, the property owned by the Church grew also, as did the numbers of lay-people living within the boundaries. This growth of proto-towns needed a legal administra-

tion, and the monks began the transcription of the Brehon laws into written Irish, becoming proficient in both canon and civil law. The copying of manuscripts was a part of this professional training but not a popular part, because bored comments were often scribbled in the margins.

Although Bardic schools had existed since pagan times, it was from the 12th century onwards that education became somewhat formalised within the monastic system. Churches with schools attached included Drogheda and Kilmallock, Co. Limerick, founded in the 13th century, Gowran, Co. Kilkenny, founded in 1312, and Scattery Island off County Clare, by 1400. The friary of the Hermits of St. Augustine at Callan, Co. Kilkenny was famous for its collection of early manuscripts. Leighlin in County Carlow also had a school attached to the church and in 1458 it was reported that the Prior, Milo Roche, 'was more addicted to the study of music and poetry than was

The tomb of Piers FitzOge Butler, in Kilcooley Abbey, Co. Tipperary carved in 1526 by Ireland's greatest medieval sculptor, Rory O'Tunney.

fit.' From the 14th century attempts were made to establish universities and St. Patrick's University was founded at the Cathedral in Dublin in 1310. It failed after ten years because of lack of government support. Its Grammar School, founded in 1489, continues today. Lismore in County Waterford was an important school in the 12th century and under Malchus, a Benedictine, was the most advanced and important centre of learning and culture in Ireland for over four decades. [de Breffny, 1976] There was a proposal to establish a university in Drogheda in 1465, but Tiptoft, the lord deputy at the time, scotched the idea.

Irish students were attending Oxford by the beginning of the 13th century and studying law at the London Inns of Court. The Irish were attending medical school in France and Italy in the

early 14th century. Numbers continued to grow at Oxford, despite misgivings in the English parliament about educating England's 'enemies', and in 1333 Dundalk-born Richard FitzRalph became chancellor of that university. A statute was passed in 1413 attempting to limit the numbers of Irishmen attending Oxford but with little effect, because a famous tutor, Mathew O'Howen, lectured there for 14 years. The sons of northern chiefs tended to travel to the University at Glasgow, founded in 1420.

The 12th-century Lavabo, or wash-house, of Mellifont Abbey, dissolved in 1536, converted into a private house and ultimately dismantled.

Old traditions die hard, and the inter-provincial rivalry between Connacht and Ulster flared up in Rome in 1466, when 'Teig Duff Mac Gillacoisgle took the *eric* [fine] of Cuchulainn from the Connachtmen in Rome.' This rowdy contest reverberates back to the *Táin Bo Cuailigne* of 700 years before! [Nicholls, 1972]

By 1539 it was reported that six monasteries taught 'vertue, learnyng and the English tonge and behaviour.' Of these, half were in Dublin – for girls, the Nunnery of Grace Dieu and, for boys, perhaps a choice, St. Mary's Abbey where Capel Street is now, Christ Church and a house of the White Monks (Cistercians). Kildare had a monastic school in Greatconnell and a collegiate school was founded at St. Brigid's Cathedral about 1500. These named monasteries were the subject of an appeal against their suppression since they were highly regarded as schools in their own right and their closing would reduce the ability of the Crown to educate the Irish in English ways, although this was a forlorn hope by the late 16th century.

The dissolution of the monasteries in the 16th century resulted in the destruction and loss of countless manuscripts and the removal of access to education for many of the population. The contents, comprising the personal possessions of the monks and friars and the communion plate and processional crosses, had been valued at over £100,000 sterling, but in the rush to acquire the properties, only a fraction of this sum was realised. [Maxwell, 1923]

As the monasteries were taken over, the contents of the libraries were sold wholesale to European dealers or, according to John Bale, Protestant Bishop of Ossory, the pages of vellum were used by the new owners to 'rub their boots or scour their candlesticks'. [O'Neill, 1984] The monastic buildings were often broken down and demolished, to the horror and outrage of the former parishioners. Although Henry VIII had promised the Dean of St. Patrick's Cathedral that the surrender of its lands would provide the funds for a university, his successor, Edward VI, kept the money and no college was established. In 1570, Sir Philip Sidney made an attempt to revive the earlier St. Patrick's University and offered land and cash, but dissent between the Dublin archbishops and the promoters caused the idea to lapse. A university was proposed for Clonfert in 1581, but came to nothing. The principle was to keep the people from information and, as a letter from a Jesuit priest to the Pope states, 'the [policy] was deliberately contrived to keep the natives in the gloom

of barbarous ignorance and thus retain them as slaves in abject obedience'. [Stopford-Green, 1908]

By the early 17th century, conditions in the country precluded the
production of elaborate manuscripts, and the work of the Four
Masters is in a hurried style, compared with the elaborate hand used
before. As Gaelic civilisation collapsed, the urgency was to record
what was left, rather than create anything new.

TOWNS AND CITIES
KILKENNY

A king of Osraighe in the 9th century, Cerball mac Dunlainge, found
that by dominating the river valleys of the Barrow and the Nore, he
could control the Viking forays into Leinster. By a combination of
tactics, bribery and manipulation, he succeeded in controlling the
Norse of south Leinster from 870 until his death in 888. He married
his daughter into the Dublin Vikings and acted as 'protector' of the
Dubliners for an annual fee. Cerball, like many Irish nobles of that
time and later, found that it was far more profitable to exact tribute
from the Norse of the towns than levy sub-kings with all the conse-
quent possibilities of treachery and non-payment.

The city of Kilkenny began as a town around the castle of
William the Marshall in 1204. The castle was bought by James Butler,
3rd Earl of Ormond in 1391 and the town remained important
through Butler patronage for several centuries. [Harbison, 1970]

The Butlers had been tied to the interests of England through having young heirs being made wards of court and educated in England,
but by 1406 they were marrying into Irish noble families, and
MacRisteard Butler, son of an O'Reilly mother and captain of his
nation, married an O'Carroll of Ely in the Cathedral of St. Canice in
1419. He was impeached in 1421 on the charge that he was appointing
Irishmen to important posts in the Church and not preferring
Englishmen, in defiance of a statute of 1416. Nevertheless, he commissioned the scribe O'Clery to write a book of psalms for Archbishop

This tower of Kilkenny castle dates to the 13th century and by local tradition was used to imprison both Alice Kyteler, the infamous 'witch,' and Bishop Ledrede, her persecutor.

The vast monastery of Athassel, Co Tipperary was founded in the late 12th century by a de Burgh and its shattered remains cover over 4 acres. Dedicated to St Edmund, its church is nearly 210ft long and is entered through an elaborate doorcase, above which hung the great crucifix of the monastery. [Leask, 1955]

O'Hedigan of Cashel as a gift for the tuition he had received from the archbishop when he was a young man.

Later, Butlers began the school in Kilkenny in c.1538 and the then Earl of Ormond, a member of the Dublin parliament, was able to translate its speeches into Irish. His successor was suspected of being involved in the Geraldine rebellion of 1546 and was secretly poisoned while visiting London; his dying wish was that his heart be buried in Kilkenny. [Stopford-Greene, 1908]

Kilkenny came to prominence again in 1641 when the Catholic Old English of Ireland established a representative assembly to negotiate with the government in Dublin over the Northern rebellion. The Confederates' position was complicated by the civil war that broke out in England in 1642 and the execution of Charles I in 1649.

Although the cities of Cork, Waterford, Limerick and Galway were independent, owing to their charters, they were viewed with suspicion by the Gaelic lords of their districts, who saw them as satellites of English power and administration. The

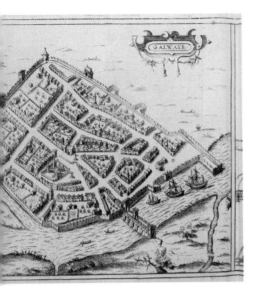

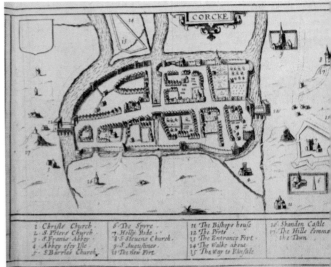

1. Christs Church.   6. The Spyre.   11. The Bishops house   16. Shanden Castle
2. S. Peters Church   7. Hellj Rode .   12. The Pirts   17. The Hille Commo
3. S. Francis Abbey   8. S Steuens Church.   13. The Entrance Fort   the Town
4. Abbey ofty Ile   9. S. Augustines.   14. The Walke about
5. S Barries Church.   10 The new Fort   15. The Way to Kinsale

population of the towns remained small throughout the medieval period and those population figures available suggest around 2,000 people each for the towns of Bantry, Baltimore, Drogheda, Dundalk, Sligo, Trim and Youghal. [Sheehan, 1986]

Maps showing the walled Cities of Galway, Cork and Limerick. drawn by Georgious Braun, c.1572. Courtesy of University College Cork.

A 15th/16th-century tomb in Jerpoint Abbey, Co. Kilkenny, founded in the twelfth century by Donal MacGillapatrick, King of Ossory.

A pamphlet printed in 1586 exhorting gentlemen from Dorset, Somerset, Devon, Lancashire and Cheshire to take land in the plantation of Munster, showed such prices as, 'A fresh salmon, costing 10 shillings in London, here for 6d, 30 eggs or a fat hen for 1d, a red deer without the skin, 2s 6d, a fat beef for 13s 4d and a fat sheep for 18d'. The pamphlet, similar to mid 20th century brochures for emigrating to Australia, went on to praise the 'great store of wild swans, cranes, pheasants, partridges ... quails can be had for 3d a dozen, a dozen woodcocks for 4d and a heifer with a calf for 20 shillings'. The promotional literature concluded by saying, 'You may keep better house in Ireland for fifty pounds a year than for two-hundred in England'. [Maxwell, 1923]

88

WATERFORD CITY

By 1567, Waterford was considered to be the second city in Ireland and contained nearly 1,000 houses within its walls. These walls, almost a mile in circumference, had 17 towers, all with cannon and gates controlling access. Its atmosphere, described as 'close' by reason of 'thick buildings and narrow streets', must have been similar to walled cities across Europe, bustling, smelly, loud and occasionally violent. Richard Stanihurst described the inhabitants as 'sharp witted, pregnant in conceiving [full of ideas], quick in taking and sure in keeping.' When choosing their mayor, they respected 'not only his riches, but his experience', and while being 'cheerful in the entertainment of strangers', they despised laziness and were 'addicted to thriving'.

The city traded with Galicia in northern Spain, and with

Early shipping from the 11th century. [*Knights Engravings of Old England*, 1845.]

89

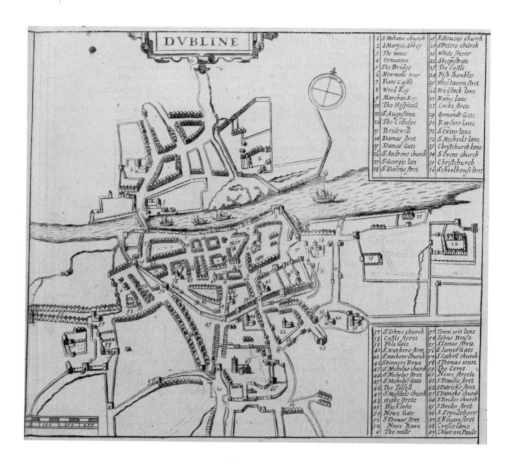

DVBLINE

1	S Mihans church	19	S Stevens church
2	S Maryes Abbey	20	S Peters church
3	The inner	21	White freers
4	Ormunten	22	Sheep streete
5	The Bridge	23	The Castle
6	Newmans tour	24	Fish shambles
7	Fians Castle	25	Whit tavern streit
8	Wood Key	26	Wodstock lane
9	Marchan Key	27	Raine lane
10	The Hospitall	28	Cocke strete
11	S Augustinz	29	Ormonds Gatt
12	The Colledge	30	Kaysars Lane
13	Bridewill	31	S Owens lane
14	Damas stret	32	S Michaels lane
15	Damas Gate	33	Christchurch lane
16	S Andrews church	34	S Owens church
17	S Georges lan	35	Christchurch
18	S Stevens stret	36	Scheelhouse lane

37	S Iohns church	53	Tenni cort lane
38	Castle streit	54	S Iohns House
39	Pole Gate	55	S Iames strete
40	S Warbers stret	56	S Iames Gate
41	S Warbers church	57	S Cathvē church
42	Skinners Rowe	58	S Thomas court
43	S Nicholas church	59	The Come
44	S Nicholas stret	60	Newe strecte
45	S Nicholas Gate	61	S Francus strect
46	The Tollsell	62	S Patricks stret
47	S Michaels church	63	S Patricks church
48	Highe strete	64	S Brides church
49	Back lane	65	S Brides stret
50	Newe Gate	66	S Seepulchers
51	S Thomas stret	67	S Keuam stret
52	Newe Rowe	68	Crosse lane
*	The mille	69	Churon Pauls

Map of Dublin, c. 1572, by Georgious Braun. [Courtesy of University College Cork]

Portugal, Andalucia and the towns of the Bay of Biscay, exporting salted fish, hides, salted meat and, in season, wheat and barley. The citizens traded with the countryside, buying the raw materials from the Gaelic people and selling them manufactured goods. Two of the specialities that Waterford was famous for were *aqua vitae* (whiskey) and quilted rugs, enormous woven fleece overcoats, popular in England and sold as 'Waterford Rugs'. The only danger from these huge coats is that they made the wearer look like a grizzly bear. One customer was almost eaten by mastiffs when he attended a bear- baiting in London and the dogs mistook him for their prey.

By 1626, Waterford had enough tailors, saddlers, hat-makers, haberdashers, hosiers, embroiderers and button-makers living within the city to demand the establishment of a Fraternal Guild, with a master, two wardens and other officials to oversee the continuation of the trades and crafts. Twice yearly, the merchants of Waterford travelled to the Great Fair of Bristol and brought back pottery, iron goods and salt. The value in taxes levied on the exports and imports of Waterford was estimated at £30,000 sterling in 1611.

DUBLIN

Dublin, or Dubh-Linn as it was known during the 8th century, had a small population of Gaelic and probably Anglo-Saxon traders and farmers. According to tradition Rumann, son of Colman, described as being 'adept in wisdom, chronology and poetry', visited the settlement in 746 and was moved to write poems for the 'Gaill' or foreigners of Ath-Cliath. When it came to payment, Rumann suggested a fee of two pinginns [pence] from every good man and one pinginn from every bad one. He got well paid. [Haverty, 1860) The same Rumann also mentions that Constantine, a Saxon king, renounced his throne and became a monk at Rahan in what is now County Offaly, bringing with him a number of Saxons to establish a community. Other Saxon foundations were in Counties Laois, Tipperary and Mayo.

The origins of the city proper go back to around the year AD 841, when Norwegian Vikings established a pirate trading port called Dyfflin near a raised wicker walkway across the mudflats of the Liffey. Despite battles, losses, expulsions and recoveries, the Viking city of Dublin was for over 200 years as important as York (Yorvik), their city in England. The Norse were joined around 852 by Danish Vikings under Olaf the White, who constructed a fortified settlement along the ridge where Christ Church and Dublin Castle now stand. He was joined by Ivar the Boneless, so called for his lack of ardour for women, who was instrumental in the Danish conquest of much of England. By 871 Dyfflin had become Dyfflinarskiri, stretching from Leixlip to

Clondalkin, where Olaf, now King of Dublin, had built himself a large timber house. He was succeeded by his son, Ivar MacAuliffe, who took the Dublin Vikings on several raids to the North of England.

The Norse state continued to grow, establishing Arklow and Wicklow and consolidating the Norse hold on Dyfflin. It was Godfry, son of Ivar, who retook the city after its capture by the Leinstermen in 917, and his son Reginald MacIvar defeated a huge force of the Irish under the King of Tara, Niall Black-Knee, at the Battle of Islandbridge in 919. Another MacIvar became king of the Danes of Waterford and by 989, after umpteen battles between the Danes and Irish, a tribute was agreed between the Danes and Malachy, the High King, to comprise 'an ounce of gold payable out of every capital messuage and garden in Dublin, payable at Christmas, to him and his successors for ever'.

Dyfflin gradually became Gaelicised and, in 999, Viking warriors offered to fight for Leinster against the claimed High King, Brian Ború. Other kings felt that Brian Ború was a usurper, not of a long and distinguished lineage, who had no right to levy tributes on any-one. Ború took Dublin that year and, according to the annals, carried away considerable amounts of gold and silver and enslaved the Dubliners. He had become a military leader through long campaigning against the Vikings of Limerick and knew when and how to fight. The Leinster kings revolted against Brian Ború's claimed domination again in 1013, and, along with their Viking allies, were finally defeated at Clontarf on Good Friday 1014. This battle, represented for so long as a defeat of a foreign enemy (the Norse) by good Christian Irishmen, was nothing of the sort. It was an attempt by the Dalcassians from Clare to grab the high kingship, and it succeeded, albeit briefly. The effort and the death of Brian reduced the power of the Dalcassians and they were no longer contenders for the crown of Ireland.

After the Battle of Clontarf, Dublin continued as before under its half-Gaelic, half-Viking king, Sigtryggr (Silkenbeard) MacAuliffe. The dimensions of the tiny Viking 'city' were about the size of a football arena. Its high-banked, wicker-fenced walls were surrounded by green fields to the north and west and mudflats to the east. Sigtryggr was a capable leader and created Ireland's first coinage. He decided to become a Christian, and after he was baptised went on pilgrimage to Rome in 1028; he founded Christ Church cathedral on his return. He died in 1036 and the Viking influence gradually declined, their kings now being earls under Irish Leinster kings.

In 1163, Dermot MacMurrough founded the monastery of St. Mary de Hogge, where Trinity College now stands and an Augustinian priory in 1163 when his brother-in-law, Laurence O'Toole, was Archbishop of the growing city. In 1166, Dublin acknowledged Rory O'Conor as High King and helped expel Dermot. When Dermot returned in 1171, he brought his Norman allies.

The majority of the Normans fought mounted, protected by hauberks, skirted coats of steel rings, while their Welsh archers, wore byrnies, leather quilted jackets reinforced with studs. Most wore conical steel helmets. They understood ambush and night attack, relishing the elements of military strategy, and struck the

Irish like a steel battering ram. They took most of Leinster with less than 2,500 men and their Irish allies.

Miles de Cogan, ancestor of the Gogans, won the first battle of Dublin in 1171 beneath the earthen walls where present-day Dame Street rises toward Christ Church. The battle for possession of the Viking city was long and bloody, with many men limbless and decapitated by the battle-axe of the Viking leader, John the Madd. The contest was won by de Cogan's strategy of sending his brother Richard circling around the battlefield and attacking the Norse from the rear. The armoured cavalry of the Normans crashed into the Vikings and they broke and fled. Their earl, Haskulf, was caught and killed. The Normans occupied the city in triumph.

The second battle occurred later that summer when the High King Rory O'Conor blockaded the city with a huge army consisting of MacDunlevy of Ulidia, O'Rourke of Breffni, O'Carroll of Oriel and O'Melaghlin of Meath, intending to starve the Normans into surrender. They didn't. After two futile months, Rory encamped at Castleknock to consider what to do next. The Normans did not wait. On a warm September afternoon, they left Dublin in three groups of about 700 knights each. They moved quickly across the Liffey toward Finglas and down the Tolka valley behind where the Phoenix Park is now. They struck the Irish camp from the rear and the left flank in a devastating surprise attack. The knights and archers destroyed the Irish forces and by nightfall Dublin was Norman. [Hayes-McCoy, 1969]

Strongbow died in 1176, of 'a mortification of the foot', brought on, according to popular lore, by St. Brigid, whose churches he had desecrated. He was buried in Christ Church. The Normans consolidated their hold on Dublin and the Vikings were forcibly moved to the northside of the Liffey, creating one of the first settlements outside the walls, Oxmanstown, the town of the Ostmen. This community grew northward's and displaced the Gaelenga, an Irish tribe living along the Tolka, into Meath. Eventually the Norse of Dublin intermarried with the Irish and lived on farmland running from St.

Michan's Church (Church Street) to where Glasnevin and Ballymun now stand. According to tradition their leader, Strum, lived around Stormanstown, former farmland where Collins Avenue and Ballymun Road meet. Perhaps we may conclude that whatever Viking blood has survived over the centuries is more likely to be found on Dublin's northside!

By the early 13th century, people from Bristol were forming a considerable element of Dublin's population. On Easter Monday 1209, they went as per custom to Cullenswood (now Ranelagh) for their traditional Maypole celebrations. They were ambushed by the O'Tooles and 300 were killed. The area was known as the 'Bloody Fields' until the nineteenth century and from 1209 to 1809, the Corporation of Dublin rode to the area every year to 'mark the safe bounds of the city' in commemoration of that event.

In 1348, the Black Death arrived in Dublin, killing 14,000 people between August and December. However, church building resumed after a lull and Dublin now began to grow outside the walls around another cathedral, St. Patrick's, with its accompanying Palace of St. Sepulchre. There was a leper hospital in honour of St. Stephen, a Carmelite Friary, a Dominican Friary and several parish churches. In 1395, the annals record that 'four Irish Kings, having performed their vigils and heard mass, received, with great solemnity, the honour of knighthood at the hands of King Richard II at Christ Church Cathedral and afterwards at a great celebration in the Castle'. In 1407, Henry IV granted that the mayor and his successors should carry before them a gilded sword as a mark of the great service they had done the crown. The first mayor was Roger Muton from 1229–30 and there has been a continuous succession ever since. The city continued to grow and a mint was established in 1459.

Dublin had many of the social attributes of European medieval cities by the 15th century. In particular, it had a series of Trade Guilds which performed pageants on certain Holy Days. On 21 June 1498, the Feast of Corpus Christi, a great colourful procession, like an El Salvador St. Patrick's Day Parade, proceeded 'with great commotion

Part of the 13th-century city walls behind St Audeon's church, Dublin.

and musick' to Christ Church for High Mass. A contemporary document describes the Medieval Guilds as follows: *Weavers* – as Abraham, Isaac and the lamb; *Embroiderers* – Moses and the children of Israel; *Carpenters* – Our Lady and the Holy Child; and the *Skinners* as the body of the camel upon which they sat. There was the added instruction that the *Painters* were responsible for painting the head of the camel. The Dublin Goldsmiths were the three kings of the East, the Fishmongers the twelve apostles, and the Butchers the tormentors of Christ. Every guild was represented, as were the unmarried young men of the city, who paraded in all their medieval finery of silk and crimson, with a 'Mayor of the Bull Ring', a gentleman appointed as 'Captain of the Bachelors' to ensure their good order. [Maxwell, 1923] Following a riot between some of the eminent citizens of Dublin and followers of the Earl of Kildare during Mass in May 1512, the Pope obliged the Mayor of Dublin to walk barefoot before the sacrament every Corpus Christi procession. The penance continued until the Reformation forced the ending of the procession and the feast day.

ST MARY'S ABBEY

The remains of St. Mary's Abbey, once the richest Cistercian monastery in Ireland, now lies under the buildings between Capel Street and Boot Lane. Founded in 1139, its grounds covered where Green Street Court House stands today, commemorating the original 'Fair Green' where fruit, vegetables and animals were sold throughout the medieval period. During excavations for a new bakery in the 1880s, structural walls and tiles were uncovered and a conjectural map was created, showing a large church stretching northwards from the chapter house with a cloister in front. The chapter house was used as a meeting room for the Great Council of Ireland in the 16th century and it was here that Silken Thomas, son of the Earl of Kildare, began his ill-starred rebellion. This room remains, its impressive rectangular vaulted space once lit by the now bricked-up windows in the east end. [Pearson, 2000]

16th century house and interior.
[*Knights Engravings of Old England*, 1845.]

The Reformation and the wars of the 17th century dealt many severe blows to the city. Dublin looked like a medieval city that had gone to seed. Badly walled, the metropolis was dominated by the 13th-century castle with its five towers and gatehouse. The Great Hall,

Religious mystery plays, popular across Europe in the Middle-Ages and a regular part of Dublin street life. [*Knights Engravings of Old England,* 1845.]

where the Irish parliament sat, had been burnt by a fire in 1671 and other accidental fires had damaged the rest. It was less than impressive. The city had several mansions of the great and the good, among them the house of the Great Earl of Cork, who was the equivalent of a billionaire and whose immense house stood where City Hall now stands. For entertainment, the citizens could attend the Cockpit on Wellington Quay; pubs such as The White Hart and The Bear offered wines and beers. Dublin had over 1,000 pubs by the mid-17th century. At the dissolution of the monasteries in 1539, the Priory of Friars Preachers, where the Four Courts now stands, was converted into lodgings for lawyers and, eventually became the site for the law courts. [Somerville-Large, 1979]

DUBLIN CASTLE

In 1204, a royal mandate was issued for the building of a castle on the high ground above the river Liffey. It was completed around 1228, under the supervision of Henry de Londres, Archbishop of Dublin and a Canterbury appointee. The castle was the seat of English power for 700 years and the meeting place for the Great Councils, the equivalent of a ruling committee. Usually these comprised great lords from their estates in Kildare or Limerick,

Gothic Revival pinnacles on the Chapel Royal at Dublin Castle.

Sir Henry Sidney leaving Dublin Castle with his army, with the heads of slain Irish on spikes over the gate

Sir Henry Sidney greeting Dublin Corporation in 1581. Engravings by John Derrick.

O Sydney worthy of tryple re-
nowne,
For plaguyg the traytours that
troubled the crowne. 1581.

whose allegiances were often split between the land of their birth and the land from which they drew a great deal of their power and mandate to rule. Much of the present appearance of the Castle is 18th century, although the ancient walls lie beneath the present courtyards. The river Poddle supplied the moat and the Bermingham Tower represents the original imposing scale of the walls and defences and contains a supper room. Dublin Castle was the centre of power in medieval Ireland and it housed the Offices of State and the original Parliament House, used intermittently until its destruction by fire in the 17th century.

It was in the Castle that the first Dublin play, in the modern sense of the word, was performed. A drama, replacing the old morality plays, was put on after a banquet for Sir Philip Sidney in 1569. Theatre had begun and was as astonishing as television to the people then, as groups of strolling players arrived from England, performing the equivalent of satirical sketches about political events. Dublin was becoming fashionable, and merchants went on buying trips to London to bring back the latest 'hats and swords, velvets and silks'. [Somerville-Large, 1979]

Penitents however were still dressed in white robes and hoods and a particular individual, George Bateman of Kilmainham, was forced to parade around Christ Church in white with a sign over his head that read 'For Adultirie, leaving his wyfe in England alyve and marryeng another heere'.

Other problems in Dublin were the numbers of taverns and the general traditional role of women as brewers and consequentially, tavern-keepers. This led to accusations of 'harlotry', especially from the newly arrived citizens of England, to whom such behaviour 'could do no less that procure the indignation of God against the honourable city' An innovation to cleanse the streets was the building of a 'common jakes' on Wood Quay.

The cities of Cork, Galway and Limerick were described by the traveller Fynes Morrison in 1617 as being 'of unwrought stone, or flint, or unpolished stones, two stories high and covered with tiles'.

Dublin and Waterford appear from his descriptions to be more modern, in that they were 'of timber, clay and plaster', similar, perhaps, to Elizabethan cage-work houses that have survived in large numbers in England. Some of these houses were the equivalent of B&Bs with a charge equivalent to 12p (15cent) per night! The city's population was still small by English standards and has been calculated at approximately 36,000 by 1610. Around that time, a new fashion arrived from England, namely coaches for wealthy families. Their novelty caused great uproar when driven through the streets.

In later times Chichester House, a mansion that stood where the Bank of Ireland now stands on College Green, became the seat of the Irish Parliament it had two houses, Commons and Lords, and entry was through a gate between guardhouses into a courtyard with the houses of that parliament on either side. Dublin's population had grown to about 69,000 by 1682.

MEDIAEVAL WOMEN

The position of women is a good test by which a civilization or a country may be judged, and that position is a combination of theory, legal position and everyday experience. In Ireland at the present moment, women are achieving parity, at least in numbers, in some universities, but this has taken years to come about. In general, women have had a slow emergence from many years of second-class citizenship. However, it was during the Middle Ages, at least 500 ago, when the legal, social and almost human definition of Woman was formed. During that era, women in Ireland were seen but not frequently heard, expected to be obedient to their husbands and to bring up children. Then, opinion-makers came from two places – the Church and the aristocracy – so women in general had no public voice. Ideas about them were formed by (mostly) celibate priests or the Gaelic lords, a particularly narrow social caste who saw women as an ornamental asset, subordinate to the family business, namely land. Some men, however, made gifts of land to their wives and perhaps in order to avoid giving away anything personal, two 14th-century bishops of Raphoe in County Donegal are on record as having generously pledged lands belonging to the See to their wives for this purpose. [Nicholls, 1973]

Ordinary common folk, the women who worked the land alongside labouring men, heard on Sundays that women were the very gates of hell; Eve betrayed humanity, but Mary was Queen of Heaven. Real women were bad, celestial virgins were good. [Kearney, 1997]

We could say, therefore, that popular theories about women and their nature came from people entirely unfamiliar with the great mass of womankind and it was those prejudiced elites, Irish Church and Irish nobility, who defined marriage and the status of women under the law. And if women today are representative of happier times, no longer tied by biology or dogma to the roles of mother and maidservant, it is all the more extraordinary to find in medieval Ireland, despite the prevalent anti-women ideas of that male society, unique women who defied subordination and whose courage against orthodoxy in a narrow-minded era marks them out as special.

FINOLA MacDONNELL (Ineen Dubh) born c.1548

Most medieval women had their lives determined for them, but not all. A very different kind of woman was the Lady of Donegal Castle, Ineen Dubh O'Donnell, who combined a Machiavellian grasp of Irish politics with a calculating sharpness of purpose.

She had been born Finola MacDonnell of Argyle and came to Ireland in 1569 to marry the O'Donnell of Tyrconnell, prince of one of Ulster's most powerful families. But instead of bringing harpists or something feminine as her dowry, she brought a substantial amount of cash and her own private army of Redshanks, Scottish warriors known from the colour of their trews or trousers. Ineen's Scottish mercenary army ensured her personal respect as the wife of a prince, and her son, Red Hugh O'Donnell, travelled with his mother's mercenaries at all times. He was engaged to the daughter of the O'Neill of Tyrone and this major political/society wedding would unite the two most influential families of Ulster, creating a power base that England wanted to prevent at any cost. Her first challenge came when Red Hugh was kidnapped by English spies, who had hidden aboard a wine merchant's ship. He was taken to the dungeons of Dublin Castle to join Art O'Neill, his future brother-in-law. He would probably have been moved to the Tower of London, to die a prisoner, because, alive, he was potentially dangerous.

However, Ineen Dubh O'Donnell was a woman of resources. She was to Donegal what Catherine Medici was to Renaissance Italy – cultured, intelligent and capable of any act deemed necessary for survival. She knew the dangerous politics of the time and, like a mafia don, could smile as she stuck a dagger in your back. Her character was again put to the test when Hugh O'Gallagher attempted to replace her son while he was in chains in Dublin Castle. She had O'Gallagher murdered in 1588. Her husband's mental state seemed to have been in decline and Ineen became the most powerful individual in Tyrconnell. In 1590, she was personally involved in the defeat of another pretender, Donnell O'Donnell, while endlessly petitioning the authorities in London and Dublin to have her son

released. He eventually escaped with her help and the influence of Hugh O'Neill, Earl of Tyrone. The political high point of this resolute and formidable woman's life was probably at Kilmacrennan in 1592 when her son, Red Hugh, was inaugurated as The O'Donnell.

Despite the Plantation of Ulster and the subsequent Flight of the Earls, Ineen remained in Ulster, declining to emigrate to Spain with the rest of the Ulster Gaelic aristocracy. Ineen Dubh O'Donnell was granted 600 acres from the O'Donnell's huge land holdings and lived out the rest of her life as a quiet country landowner of modest estate. [Connolly, 1998]

Rockfleet Castle, Co. Mayo was the scene for a victory in 1574 for the pirate queen Grace O'Malley against Captain William Martin and a party of troops from Galway intent on stopping her piratical activities. After almost three weeks of siege, Grace rallied her sailors and soldiers and drove Martin back to Galway, greatly enhancing her status as leader of the O'Malleys. [Chambers, 1979]

GRACE O'MALLEY (c.1530-1603)

Being a chieftain in the 16th century was really a man's job – nasty, brutish and short. Few survived middle age. But one of the longest-lasting and most effective chieftains of Ireland was a woman – Grace O'Malley – and she was formidable. She was someone who did not trouble herself about the boundaries imposed by society, and her character comes across in the fine biography by Anne Chambers.

Described by the Elizabethan Philip Sidney as 'a most famous feminine sea-captain', she was the daughter of Dubhdara O'Malley, Lord of Upper Umhall, and lived an independent and free life with castles at strategic points along the Mayo coast. The largest, on Clare Island, was built in the late 15th century and the island also has an abbey containing some of the most important medieval frescoes in Ireland. The surrounding drumlins of Clew Bay provided an ideal hiding place for her pirate ships which traded from Scotland to Spain.

The O'Malleys were an important family in Connacht in the Middle Ages and had many sources of income; in particular, any-thing to do with the ocean. Claiming ownership of the western seas, Grace rented out the rich fisheries to Spanish boats and charged all others for sailing through O'Malley waters. Renting the fisheries was an established business for the O'Malleys and they may have had a small ship-building industry to facilitate the management of the resource. With her fast pirate galleys, Grace extorted a percentage of the cargo from the merchant carracks sailing for Galway, boarding them with her sailors and taking what she wanted. However, the O'Malley piracy possibly had a detrimental effect on the long-term viability of Galway trade. [Brady and Gillespie, 1986]

Grace was married twice, first to an O'Flaherty and subsequent-ly to the chief of the Mayo Burkes, and the Burke castle of Rockfleet on Clew Bay was where she spent most of her time. While it seems bare and uncomfortable to the modern eye, it would have been quite comfortable in its day, with fires lit and tapestries adorning the walls. It was probably from Rockfleet that she sailed to London in 1593, a round-trip of perhaps 1,000 nautical miles, to meet Elizabeth I, as queen to queen and woman to woman. The purpose of this meeting was to resolve some of the problems she was experiencing with the governor of Connacht, Richard Bingham, and his encroachments on O'Malley lands. She succeeded in obtaining a legal grant of a portion of her divorced husband's estate, in defiance of existing Brehon Law. Her correspondence with Elizabeth shows her to have been a person of intelligence and insight, more than capable of negotiating with those of superior force and resources.

Perhaps as a result of this meeting, Grace became more aware than other Irish clan leaders that England's power was growing and that the old ways were no longer enough, especially against administrators like Bingham, who used fire and the sword to achieve what the law could not. As a shrewd observer of Elizabethan England, she was one of a number of Gaelic rulers who sought accommodation with the authorities. Her sons were among the Gaelic lords who fought against O'Neill at Kinsale and although this could appear as some form of betrayal to contemporary nationalist eyes, it was a pragmatic move that Grace herself would have approved.

ALICE KYTELER born c.1304

Dame Alice Kyteler is not a heroine in the mould of Grace O'Malley or Ineen Dubh, but she allows the 21st-century reader to enter the irrational and paranoid world of the medieval clerical mind. The Kyteler witchcraft case set the precedent for other similar trials in later centuries, including an incident in 1578, again in Kilkenny, when three people were tried and burnt, including an unfortunate described as a 'blackamoor'. [Somerville-Large, 1975] The Kyteler case set out the legal grounds for linking sorcery and heresy, which gave the church authorities more leeway for prosecuting and, following her trial, the legal precedents were used against Adam Duff O'Toole, who was burnt in Hoggen, now College Green, Dublin, in 1327 for saying that the Bible was a fable and that Mary, the mother

of Jesus, was a tart. Others followed in 1352 for similar insults to clerical authority, although in general Ireland was not a place of systematic persecution.

The 14th century was, however, a time of terror and superstition.
People believed that Satan was out and about and that magic spells
caused diseases and changed the weather. It was a fearful time, compounded by shortages of food, recurring plague and a general feeling of impending apocalypse. The Church as an institution was also
in trouble. The Papacy had become a secular power, with mistresses
and an art collection. Christianity had failed to prevent or explain
war, famine, plague or, indeed, the Church's great wealth when the
majority were poor. People were beginning to question its claims of
divine guidance and its authority was declining. But an effective way
of reasserting that dominance and distracting people from their real
problems was to find a scapegoat to blame. Pope John XXII became
obsessed with heresy and witchcraft, seeing anything unorthodox as
a challenge to the Church's supremacy. Women, in particular,
became the target for that outwardly projected paranoia.

Ireland was relatively free of this demented misogyny, but in 1324
there was an inquisition against Dame Alice Kyteler in Kilkenny that
set the standard for others who followed. The man behind it was
Bishop Richard Ledrede, a zealous believer in Church authority.
While Kyteler is not a particular example of radical feminism, she
and her unfortunate servant, Petronella, illustrate the extreme punishment that was used to threaten people into subjection.

Ledrede was a deeply unpopular man almost from the time he
arrived in Kilkenny as Bishop. As an English Franciscan, he was called
an 'Alien and a Vagabond' by the people of Kilkenny and he fell out
with most of the important citizens, especially the Senechal or Chief
Steward, Arnold le Poer. It may have been this feud that caused him
to target Alice Kyteler, le Poer's friend, as a way of reducing the
Senechal's position. But Alice Kyteler was not without suspicion. She
had been married four times, her first three husbands having died of
an illness that today suggests arsenic poisoning. The fourth was los-

Gowran church, Co. Kilkenny houses the 14th century cenotaph of Eleanor de Bohun, niece of Edward III of England, wife of James le Botellier, early founder of the Butler family.

ing his hair and nails and seemed to be heading the same way, which looked more than coincidence. She had three sons by her previous husbands and they accused her of sorcery. Ledrede decided this was an ideal case to assert his authority.

To the medieval clerical mind, sorcery and heresy were closely related since both implied a rejection of the Church's authority. To be accused of witchcraft was bad but heresy was worse. Combining the two would have been lethal for Alice. Her sons produced 'evidence', a box containing what they said were dead men's nails, spiders, deformed worms and the brains of unbaptised dead children. They accused Alice of boiling this Hell's Kitchen recipe in the skull of a decapitated thief. For dessert, according to her accusers, Alice sacrificed nine red cockerels and munched peacocks' eyes. The obligatory broomstick was also found. Witnesses said that she used to 'gallop through thick and thin'.

Bishop Ledrede had Alice, her servant Petronella, her favourite son William and a group of acquaintances charged and tried for witchcraft and sorcery, but Arnold le Poer locked up the 'alien from England' as he described him, until the trial date had passed. But the bishop was determined and eventually persuaded the authorities in Dublin to rein-state the charges. Dame Alice escaped, with the help of rich relatives, and disappeared to England. The bishop was furious and ordered that Petronella be tortured to exact a confession. She was whipped and beaten until she confessed to whatever they wanted her to say and on 13 September 1325, innocent Petronella, originally from County Meath, was dragged through the streets and burned as a witch in the high street in Kilkenny. [Somerville-Large, 1975]

By asserting that women were in league with Satan, having sex with demons and other bizarre unprovable acts, the Church could claim that the so-called 'evils' of society, disease, famine or whatev-er, were emanating from these usually poor and isolated individuals, and burn them alive as heretics and witches. Contriving through tor-ture to have them confess before being burnt enabled the imagined 'evil' to disappear in smoke and allowed the Church to re-establish itself as a commanding champion in a wicked world. Countless thousands of women died in this grotesque manner across Europe during the medieval period.

MARGARET OF OFFALY, died 1451

Today, many rich women are patrons of the arts. They attend opera or collect paintings, become authorities on post-modernism or 17th-century composers and, through their financial support, often bring young and aspiring artists to a wider audience. And since the arts today are additionally supported by government subventions, active women artists arguably have more opportunities and a wider and wealthier buying public than ever before.

When we attempt to explore theories of art and beauty in the medieval period, especially in Ireland, there is very little material to work on because so much was destroyed through war and pillage; few examples, except ruined buildings, exist to show us what was there to begin with.

But from that time, one name has survived in association with the arts, a special woman who gave of her time and money to supporting poets and musicians in a period of dire need. She was Margaret, wife of Calvagh O'Connor-Faly, a leading nobleman of Offaly. She is associated with Leap Castle, where her family, the O'Carrolls, were lords of a huge area south of the Sliabh Blooms.

In the 15th century, women of any public profile were rare, usually living a restricted and circumscribed life defined by Church and family. But Margaret O'Connor-Faly combined her interest in the arts with philanthropy and met a real social need at the same time. During a time of dire famine, she invited all the learned of Ireland to a great festival, a combination of *feis ceol* and a barbecue. They brought their families, friends and also others in need. The event took place at Killeigh, County Offaly on St. Sinchell's Day, 26 March 1433, at or around where the church originally stood. It is now incorporated into the Church of Ireland parish church and fragments in the immediate locality probably relate to the medieval nunnery and a Franciscan friary, both founded by the O'Connor-Faly family. As the famine continued that year, Margaret gave another sumptuous feast at Rathangan, an old O'Connor-Faly ring-fort in Kildare, and adopted two children orphaned because of the famine. Between the two feasts, more than 5,000 were fed, their names recorded by the Brehon MacEgan on an attendance roll for posterity. No one was excluded and those in greatest need, the destitute and poor, were given money and food to bring home.

In the custom of the time, to show that she understood the relationship between the aesthetics of culture and a religious belief summarised by the Benedictine Alcuin as *species pulchras, dulces sapores, sonos suaves* – 'it is easier to love beautiful creatures, sweet scents and lovely sounds than love God' – Margaret gave a gift of two chalices of gold to the Augustinian church founded by the O'Connor-Falys. The holy well of Killeigh still attracts pilgrims. [Stopford-Greene, 1908; de Breffni and ffolliott, 1975; Eco, 1986]

CASTLE LIFE

Within those castles of the Gaelic and Norman-Irish aristocracy, things could get a little crowded in the evenings. Everybody retired to his/her castle at night and each floor became a dormitory. The inside of the castle was a little world of its own with the lower rooms of the grooms and servants lit by tallow (sheep-fat) candles, with straw for bedding. Higher up the tower, the Gaelic lord's bedroom, lit by beeswax, was probably shared with foster children from a neighbouring lord, his own children, his wife and sometimes his mother-in-law.

The most important retainers would also sleep in the tower house at night and those of lesser status 'camped' in the passageways and stairways, while men-at-arms kept watch on the battlements. According to the historian Stanyhurst, writing in 1585, most of the castles had dining halls attached where the day-to-day business was conducted. The castles themselves were used for sleeping only. Most were unadorned in terms of decorative plasterwork, but Bunratty in County Limerick and Granagh, built on the river Suir by the le Poers, both had decorative vine-leaf motifs, with Granagh having an additional St. Michael and the Archangel relief on the wall of its dining hall. Remains of decorative plasterwork also adhere to the shell of the dining hall at Aughnanure, the O'Flaherty castle on the western shores of Lough Corrib. Although later than the medieval period, a French traveller, Monsieur Bouillaye le Gouz, described the interior of some towers as having 'little furniture; they cover their rooms with rushes, of which they make beds in the summer and straw in the winter'. [Leask, 1955].

But castles were intimate places and this style of living meant that information was passed from mouth-to-mouth. Personal contacts and integrity were more important than anything that could be committed to paper. Gossip was as essential an ingredient to communal living then as it is today. But the Middle Ages were a dangerous time, when the borders of the chieftain's territories were being tested by English troops from the Pale and his land surveyed and

measured without his permission. The gradual shiring of the independent Gaelic territories from the 14th century onwards inevitably reduced the freedom of action that the 'Captains of their nations' had traditionally enjoyed. A certain degree of paranoia would have been normal in the Irish tower house.

Urlingford Castle, 16th-century seat of the Mountgarret branch of the Butler family.

At the poorer level, people lived in beehive huts made of hides or mud over a willow frame and sat on low timber benches or rushes, a kind of uncut-Tintawn, but in the finer castles, meals were taken together at long tables. 'Trenchers', bread cut along the length, were used as plates and sometimes these trenchers were collected after the meal for the poor or prisoners. That staple of the diet, the cup of tea, was appearing as 'China Ale' in Dublin by the end of the 17th century.

The Irish chieftains were aware of the usefulness of castles, and the O'Conors took over the large castle built by Richard de Burgh at

Ballintubber, Co. Roscommon around 1300. It remained intermittently in various O'Conor hands until 1652.

The 7th Earl of Desmond built a massive banqueting hall with a slated roof covering a room 72 feet by 31 feet at Askeaton, County Limerick between 1440 and 1449. It had finely carved windows on three sides, with detail similar to the FitzGerald endowed friary nearby. The FitzGeralds built similar banqueting halls at Newcastle West, also in County Limerick, and in 1583 these were described as being surrounded by gardens and a fishpond. The O'Rourkes of Breffni (present-day Leitrim) also had a great hall at Dromahair, where they listened to petitions from tenants and officiated at the day-to-day business of their landholdings. This great structure was quarried by Sir William Villiers in 1630 to build Dromahair Castle. [de Breffni and Mott, 1976]

Birch woodland like this near Muckross, Co. Kerry would have provided perfect cover for the wild boar, deer and wolves of medieval Ireland.

Oakwoods near Abbeyleix, ancient territory of the O'Mores, dispossessed in the 16th-century plantation of Leix and Offaly.

WOODLAND

In the early 14th century, Ireland still had huge areas of woodland, unlike England where it has been estimated that forest cover was less than 15 per cent at this time. Troops attempting to force their way to a Gaelic lord's hideout had to hack through dense woodland, with pathways blocked with trenches and archers hidden behind banks on either side.

Maps of early Irish woodland show much of the east of County Roscommon to have been a large forested area, possibly extending to some hundreds of square miles. The wood, called 'The Feadha', stretched along the western shore of Lough Ree, taking in where Roscommon town is today, and continued north as far as Drumsna in Leitrim. A settlement grew from a small, forest-encircled monastery on the road between the ford at Athlone and Cruachain, the ritual site of the Connachta. It was founded in the 8th century and the county takes its name from the saint who lived there, St. Coman.

> A wall of woodland overlooks me;
> A blackbird's song sings to me
> Over my lined book the trilling of the birds sing to me.
>
> A clear-voiced cuckoo sings to me in a cloak of bush-tops;
> A lovely utterance. The Lord be good to me on judgement day!
>
> I write well under the woodland trees.
>
> *8th century, from a manuscript in the Library of St. Gall, Switzerland.*
>
> [GREENE and O'CONNOR, 1967]

To the west of the great woods was Magh Da Cheo (the plain of the mists) between Athleague and Ballyforan, which was 'a place of otherworldly associations.' Roscommon may have had trading links to the Byzantine empire as early Irish sources describe people from that empire as Romani and a townland near Dunmore, Roymonahan, is possibly the Rathromanach (fort of the Romans) later granted to the canons of nearby Kilmore by Felim O'Conor, son of Cathal of the Red Hand, in 1248. He founded a Dominican friary near to St. Coman's monastery and was buried there in 1265.

HUNTING

For recreation, the Irish aristocracy enjoyed hawking and hunting. They hunted many animals, principally red deer, venison being a welcome break from beef. The great forests that remained into the Cromwellian period contained scores of wolves and these were considered game for the chase, with a regular pack of wolfhounds being kept in County Meath by 1653. As far as farmers were concerned, wolves were nuisances and a public wolf hunt was organised in Castleknock in 1652. The Revenue Commissioners offered six pounds for the head of a she-wolf, the equivalent of a year's wages for a servant. Wolves continued to survive in Ireland long after their extinction elsewhere and the deserted copper-mines of Mount Gabriel outside Schull, Co. Cork offered a secure lair as late as 1699. Wolves were a curse to the medieval farmer and a favourite means of killing a wolf was to place fishhooks inside pieces of carrion, so that a starving wolf would gulp it down and tear itself apart. But if the wolf was to be hunted, then it was seen as another form of game, such as an otter or badger, but with different hounds. The hunters themselves included those who had been involved in the training of the hounds from their own childhood, joining the hunt from six or seven years of age. Medieval kennels were often divided into three, with a room for the hounds to sleep, a room for the kennel boy, and a 'yard' with sticks stuck into gutters in the clay for the dogs to urinate against.

The kennel boys would know every dog and bitch by colour and name and look after their welfare, making sure their sleeping area was off the ground in winter and that they had clean straw.

Horsehair would have been used as a leash to tie young and old hounds together, as a way of teaching the young how to hunt. The hounds were exercised every day and great care was taken over their condition. Thorns were a major problem for hunting dogs, so bowls of warm water were used to raise the skin before pinching the thorn. Herbs were used as laxatives if digestion was a problem.

Part of the huntsman's training was how to recognise what animal was around from its hoof prints. If they were after deer, he would know from experience whether it was a doe or a buck, whether it was in flight or walking, and whether it should be left or hunted.

The huntsman would usually leave the kennel at dawn and search for droppings and hoof prints, marking the trails as he found them, gradually building up a picture of what had been in the forest the night before. If it was to be a stag hunt, the hounds were fed bread and milk, so that they would not be too heavy for the chase.

It was the huntsman's job to manage the hounds, making sure that the lazy ones were whipped on and the keen ones held back. He would also have been responsible for the sword stroke that killed the cornered animal and the supervision of its butchery and portioning.

The stag was always skinned and quartered in a special fashion. The animal was laid stomach up on the ground and the skin cut away from the shoulders and haunches. As the skin was cut away, the stomach, testicles and kidneys were fed to the hounds, while the best joints were skewered on sharpened sticks for carrying back to the castle. Finally, the head was taken as a trophy.

Ireland remained a haven for animals long hunted to extinction elsewhere in Europe, and the pine marten, much prized for its fur in the 17th century, still exists in the West of Ireland today.

CHAPTER 6

Years of the Sword

I N THE MIDDLE AGES, right across Christendom, violence and the fear of violence was endemic. Everybody, or rather privileged males, loved fighting. And within the Gaelic system, dynastic conflict between warrior nobilities continued to be the norm. In France, Bretrand de Born, a troubadour from Perigord, sang a popular melody as he travelled from castle to castle, its lyrics not unlike our current National Anthem:

> It gives me great joy to see, knights and horses in their battle array
> My heart is filled with gladness when I see strong castles besieged
> Maces, swords, helmets of different hues, shields that will be shattered
> Horses of the dead and wounded roving at random
> Let all good men think of naught but the breaking of heads
> For it is better to die than live vanquished.'
>
> [BLOCH, 1975]

Irish warriors were fond of their food and drink, for a healthy appetite was thought to prepare the body for the next contest.

I D

Being 'large of limb', 'big-boned' and athletic required sides of boar and gallons of wine to sustain the strength. And the ability to make it all quickly disappear suggested an eagerness for the fray. But a muscular body was not enough to qualify a man as a warrior. He needed courage, and this quality – the ability to stand one's ground in the face of better armed or more numerous foes or blood-crazed Vikings – was a prized asset that every noble warrior needed. Heroism in the face of the enemy was the true mark of the knightly class in Europe, and Irish soldiers had this. They were also available at a price and fought in several English campaigns: 3,157 Irish soldiers were hired by Edward I in 1296; in 1301 he employed 1,617, and in 1335 Edward III had 1,585 Irishmen serving under the flag of St. George.

Leadership was the parallel ability required of a lord or a knight. In Ireland, the greater lords had under their command a varied collection of subsidiary nobles and their *hobelars*, the poorly equipped foot-soldiers, ever hopeful for plunder. While the Gaelic and Norman nobility did not have the resources of the great English lords, they did not lack the willpower and strength of character required to bring an army into service. There was almost no engagement between the various alliances of medieval Ireland which did not have both Gaelic and Norman-Irish troops on either side. Part of the fractured nature of Gaelic society of that time was that every Gaelic noble who was not captain of his nation, 'The O'Kelly' or 'The MacBrien', felt disinherited and slighted.

Boredom was another reason for so much bloodshed in the centuries around the first millennium. Warriors were not men of great culture, and since their social obligations were few, time could hang heavily on their hands. Ireland's warrior elite fought each other for amusement and glory. There was profit also. The loot from somebody else's land was a source of income, and cattle could be bartered for rich clothing, weapons and better horses. But as the centuries wore on and walled towns became established, the nobility looked on the merchants with amazement, as wealth seemed to be created

mysteriously, and not through blood and warfare. The towns-people were despised for their unwarlike demeanour, yet they provided a useful 'black rent', that romantic term for extortion, giving a substantial income for the Gaelic chiefs strong enough to demand it. The annual black rent paid by the shires of the Pale to the O'Byrnes in the 14th century was around 750 Irish pounds, when a soldier's wages were about three pounds a year. In today's money, it would be the equivalent of millions. The Irish nobility were not poor.

Ireland, however, is often seen as a country where a more egalitarian form of nobility existed, different to feudalism, as if the Irish chieftains were some sort of new-age-vegetarians, intent on hugging and sharing. But the Gaelic nobility was an aristocratic caste, a rul-

Fethard, Co. Tipperary was an important walled town in the Middle-Ages and its defences have been carefully restored by the Office of Public Works and local initiative.

ing elite that was as closed to serfs as any European or English variety. Vassal status in Europe was paralleled in Ireland by degrees of distance from the royal family, the *derbfine* of the ancient *tuath*. But over time, as elsewhere across Christendom, the Irish concept of nobility gradually changed from a sacred designation to a label attached to action and a mode of life. The changes affected the ownership of land as Irish noble families slowly moved from collectively owning the tuath to the land becoming 'Maguire's Country' or 'O'Cahan's Country', as the tribal designation became a family name.

IRISH SOLDIERS

In addition to the brehons, poets and associated 'professional classes' who acted as a household to the now encastellated Irish nobles of the Middle Ages, several families developed hereditary functions relating to wars and armies. The O'Donnelly family were 'marshals' to the O'Neills and the O'Connollys marshals to McMahon. The title of marshal was a military one, relating to the billeting of troops, and their fees were often the heads and hides of all cattle killed to provide victuals (cuddies) for their lord's troops.

It is difficult to find out how and what the troops of the Gaelic lords had in weapons and munitions, but a relevant document from Dublin in 1534 lists a large shipment of ordnance, sent from England to Ireland in preparation for any military eventuality. Given that there was a thriving black market in Ireland for stolen royal ordnance, perhaps some of this ended up in Irish hands. It included a demi-cannon, two brass falcons (small cannon firing a ball of about two kilos), two falconets (a ball of about one kilo), 140 cannonballs, 40 'hagbushes' (arquebuses – early firearms), saltpetre, brimstone, 500 yew bows, two barrels of bow strings, 1,000 sheaves of arrows, 300 spears, 60 great horses to pull carts, two barrels of soap, 10 horse hides, 100 felling axes, timber, nails, crowbars and miscellaneous small military and carpentry items. They all came in useful in a decade that saw the Earls of Kildare, one of Ireland's greatest families, ruined. The FitzGeralds' men-at-arms were, like so much else in Ireland, hereditary, and, as professional soldiers, they came in several types. The basic foot soldier of Irish warfare was the kerne, sometimes called wood-kerne, but this related to outlaws only. The Keatings of Kildare were the real thing, providing 160 of 'Keating's Kerne' to the Earl of Kildare, while another Keating family were captains of kerne in Tipperary. For the armed support of their sovereign liege, each man was paid a heifer every quarter year, to the value of eight shillings, and their upkeep. Their captains were paid the wages of 'Black Men', soldiers who didn't exist, approximately eight per cent of the total hire 'fees' for a band of kerne.

The elite soldiers were the gallowglasses, Hebridean Scots-Vikings, who were mainly employed in Ulster. They were of several different family groups. The Tir Conaill (Donegal) gallowglass were mainly MacSweeneys, and the first on record in Ireland was Murchadh MacSuibhne, captured in 1267 and imprisoned by the Earl of Ulster. Other Tir Conaill gallowglasses included O'Gallaghers and O'Boyles. In Tyrone, the gallowglass of O'Neill were the MacDonnells, MacConnells, MacRorys, Rogers, MacDowells, Doyles and Coyles, all claiming descent from Sumarlidi, first King of Argyle and the Hebrides. In Connacht, other families of MacDonnells, MacConnells, MacRorys and MacSweeneys formed the gallowglass of the Burkes and O'Conors. Munster had MacSheehy and Sheehan, and Leinster had MacDomhnaill and MacCabe. In return for their support, these resolute warriors received grants of land. Ultimately, over a quarter of Donegal was owned by gallowglass families and their descendants. [MacNeill, 1920]

POLITICAL AND MILITARY DEVELOPMENTS

Although the Normans had attempted to overpower the entire island, the colony was in trouble by the late 13th century. Bad weather, poor crops and a lack of sons to the ruling elite all contributed to the decline and collapse of the conquest. There were other reasons, too. More and more of the Normans were intermarrying and finding common cause with their Irish neighbours. Remoteness from England contributed to a cultural identification with Ireland, referring to themselves as 'Anglais' they never forgot their origins however. But for those in the west and south, Ireland was becoming their country as well as their home.

But there was another explanation for the decline of the colony. The Irish had learned from the Normans that tactics, the strategy of using soldiers in a purposeful way, was the key to winning battles. It was also important to have the right equipment. Up to this period, the Irish had been unable to acquire body armour, and fought in linen shirts. Very attractive in a 'Prada' sort of way but entirely useless in a battle. By the 14th century, they had the steel protection they needed.

EDWARD THE BRUCE

We think today that the 1916 Proclamation was the first time that Irish Independence was declared publicly with arms. But almost 600 years ago, Ireland, perhaps for the first time, attempted to become independent of England through electing an agreed king with an army capable of defeating the Normans and regaining control of the island.

The 14th century was when a sense of an Irish nation came to mean something in written history. The Normans had arrived in 1167 and attempted a haphazard and random conquest of large parts of the island, but within 100 years, people could see that it was not going to happen in a hurry. In 1258, a meeting was held on the banks of the Erne where the Irish kings and nobles of Connacht, Thomond and Ulster peaceably gave the high-kingship to Brian O'Neill of Tyrone. The Irish ruling classes had finally grasped a sense of solidarity, intensified by a century of military and territorial struggle. They were now fighting the Normans using gallowglass, and

Edward the Bruce's grave on Faughert Hill, near Dundalk, Co. Louth.

had improved their own military tactics. They were becoming politicised and militarily experienced. [MacNeill, 1920]

But it was when the Scots won their great victory at Bannockburn in 1314, and the English were conclusively defeated, that opportunity came to empower that growing sense of Irish independence. The victory had reawakened in the Scottish king, Robert the Bruce, a sense of kinship with the Irish which was reciprocated. He had written to the Irish kings during the winter of 1306/07 from Rathlin Island, reminding them that 'our people and your people have been free since ancient times, stem from one seed of birth and are urged to come together in love, more eagerly and joyfully by a common language and by common custom.' The Irish supported him in his recovery of his Scottish kingdom and he continued to enjoy Irish support in Ulster.

He now offered his help in the struggle against the same enemy, seeing the Irish as fellow Gaels or Celts. Around this period, a letter to Pope John XXII by the Irish nobility, in which they sought release from their obligations to Edward II as their monarch, gives an indication of their feelings:

> 'Let no person then wonder if we endeavour to preserve our lives against those cruel tyrants, usurpers of our lawful properties and murderers of our persons.... So far from thinking it unlawful, we hold it to be a meritorious act and without the least remorse of conscience, while breath remains, we shall attack them in defence of our just rights and never lay down our arms until we force them to desist.'
>
> [Remonstrance of the Irish Princes c.1315, MacGeoghegan, 1844]

Robert the Bruce of Scotland had a brother, Edward, who was ambitious, brave and available. He would have succeeded to the Scottish throne except that the victory of Bannockburn allowed Robert to swap English prisoners for his wife, who was being held hostage in England. This would produce an heir and Edward would never be king. But his availability and the sense of fellow 'Celtic' feeling between the Scots and the Irish resulted in a series of Irish campaigns from 1315 to 1318, intended to make Edward king of Ireland and Ireland free of England. Although this would deprive Scotland of valuable resources in its struggle with the English, the Bruces considered it worthwhile.

Edward arrived at Larne with a professional and triumphant Scottish army of 6,000 men on 28 May 1315 and was joined by O'Neill, O'Hagan, O'Hanlon and MacCartan. The Pope, seeking advantage in England, excommunicated all followers of the Scots, sent two cardinals to tell them to stop this war, and any monk who encouraged rebellion was to face the same excommunication. The cardinals were ignored. [Otway-Ruthven, 1980]

But Bruce had marched into the worst famine for 20 years and a lethal epidemic amongst Irish cattle. There was no food for the people and nothing at all for a starving army. Their campaigns suggest a wandering to and fro, seeking food and gaining little territory or plunder. This tactically confusing wandering, is countered by their attempt to establish a Bruce government in Ulster in opposition to the Dublin administration, although it was never effective outside the North.

There were four campaigns between 1315 and 1318. Edward's first campaign began with the sacking of Dundalk, Ardee and smaller towns. An army was raised to oppose him led by Richard de Burgo, Earl of Ulster and allies, but after a skirmish with a part of this force, Edward retreated to Coleraine and defeated a detachment led by Edmund Butler. Bruce marched south again and won another battle at Kells, Co. Meath. He was then joined by more Irish and Norman-Irish and had a victory at Ardschull, defeating the combined army of Butler and other Normans.

In 1316, Bruce returned north, taking Athy and other towns on the way and according to tradition, was crowned King of Ireland during this march at Dundalk where the Bruce Tavern now stands. He also took Carrickfergus Castle and used it as his base from then on. In this year, Gaelic leaders began making attacks on Norman power in Ireland, but the chieftains of Connacht were badly defeated at the battle of Athenry, with reports of 1,500 killed on the Gaelic side. This battle destroyed O'Conor power in Connacht and established the de Burgos as the dominant power in the west. [Dudley-Edwards, 1973]

Edward the Bruce was joined in Ireland by his brother and an army of gallowglasses. In February 1317, they marched to Castleknock, on the outskirts of Dublin, perhaps with the intention of taking the city. However, Dubliners destroyed the suburbs to deny him cover and refortified the walls by demolishing churches. By April 1317 the Bruces were, they were in Munster attempting to join forces with a faction of the O'Briens, but they returned again to Ulster and Robert the Bruce went back to Scotland. The next 18 months were quiet until Edward moved south again, to fight his last battle at Faughert, outside Dundalk. In the heat of a ferocious battle, surrounded by his enemies, Edward the Bruce was slain. His body was interred in the churchyard. [Connolly, 1998]

Edward Bruce was slain by John de Maupas, possibly a citizen of Dundalk, but it was John de Bermingham, the leader of the Anglo-Irish of Meath and Louth, who took his head to London, receiving great praise and becoming Earl of Louth. Edward's death brought an end to the Scottish involvement in Ireland for the time being; deprived Robert the Bruce of a brother and heir to the kingdom of Scotland; and stemmed the tide of Scottish expansion and ambition. Robert the Bruce came to Ireland briefly in 1328 as part of a political manoeuvring with England, but despite this visit, Scotland had no further interest in an Irish extension of its kingdom. In the period following Edward Bruce's death, England strengthened its hold on Ulster through able men such as John Athy, who controlled the Ulster coast as Admiral of the West from 1318.

Although Robert the Bruce continued to have an interest in Irish affairs after his brother's death, Scottish support for Irish independence ceased when Robert died. The real result of the Bruce invasion was that effective government control of large parts of Ireland was seriously damaged. Ulster and Connacht went their own ways and the reduction in power of the de Burgh Earl of Ulster hegemony allowed the O'Neills to emerge as the most powerful dynasty in the Middle Ages.

In England, Edward I had bankrupted the treasury with his Welsh and Scotish campaigns, leaving his successor, Edward II (see page 74) to repay the debts. After a generation of trying to pay the debts due, Edward III went to war in France and reneged on his agreements. With so little money around, Ireland was left to its own devices.

THE BATTLE OF DYSERT O'DEA

The secluded monastery of Dysert in County Clare was founded by St. Tola in the early 8th century. The church was rebuilt several times and was reconstructed in its present form by Conor O'Dea, head of the local Gaelic ruling family It has a Romanesque door case with very crisply carved heads of oriental appearance which was inserted into the south wall in 1683, at the time of its rebuilding. There is a fine high cross in an adjoining field. It was the 'family church' of the O'Deas, whose restored 15th-century castle is nearby. They were able to build the castle because of a pivotal battle fought in the previous century.

In 1276, Thomas de Clare had received from Edward I a huge grant of all the kingdom of Thomond, the historic homeland of the O'Briens. Unsurprisingly, the O'Briens fought to prevent this happening, but because of Irish succession law, different O'Briens sought to become kings of Thomond. Rival factions were aided by de Clare, eager for more territory at the expense of the O'Briens. By the early 14th century, the de Clares were in contention for taking over most of Thomond. The decade preceding the battle is a bewildering series of fragmented alliances between the O'Briens and the de Clares vs. the de

Burgos and other septs of the O'Briens, each seeking to annihilate the other and gain Thomond, but by 1318 Richard de Clare felt strong enough in arms and manpower to make his move.

The battle of Dysert O'Dea is important for several reasons. The Irish had learnt the value of tactics and armour, putting both to good use in this battle. The violent struggle between Richard de Clare and the O'Briens, O'Deas, O'Connors and O'Hehirs took place probably to the east of Ballycullinane Lough. On 10 May 1318, de Clare had decided to attack O'Brien, who had been stealing cattle as provocation. He left Bunratty Castle with about 1,000 knights and foot soldiers. Just north of Ennis, he and his men entered the country of Conor O'Dea, intending to destroy the O'Deas' main residence at Dysert. Instead, he pressed on, following some of O'Dea's men, who were driving cattle toward a large wood south of Lough Ballycullinane. The Normans chased the Irish into the outskirts of the wood and suddenly out poured the waiting Irish troops in chain mail and steel helmets under Conor O'Dea. During a brief and brutal skirmish, Richard de Clare and his advance group were killed. The Irish retreated into the woods, followed by the Normans. A desperate struggle began. The Normans were beginning to overcome the Irish when O'Hehir and O'Connor arrived with their men. The Irish joined together and the battle became a hacking, gouging bloody mass of men, swords and screams. O'Connor of Corcomroe sought out de Clare's son and they fought man to man until young de Clare fell as his father had done.

The battle, however, could still have been won by the Normans, except for the arrival of Murtough O'Brien and his army by the route-way across Spancil Hill. He could see from the smoke of burnt cabins that the Normans were ahead and his men rushed to get at the enemy. The Normans were caught between the O'Briens, O'Deas, O'Hehirs and O'Connors. Only a few escaped to Bunratty, to discover that de Clare's widow had already left, taking anything portable to Limerick for a boat back to England. Bunratty was in flames and the Norman hold on Clare was broken forever. [Hayes-McCoy, 1969]

Medieval Politics

E DWARD III was crowned King of England at the age of 14 in 1327, when the court was dominated by the arrogant Mortimer, his mother Isabella's lover and greedy claimant to Ulster and, indeed, the throne of England. By 1330, however, Edward struck and had Mortimer dragged from Isabella's bed and thrown in a dungeon. He was tried, convicted and executed for the murder of Edward II. Isabella was allowed to retire to a quiet life on a small pension at Castle Rising in Suffolk.

After the battle of Poitiers in 1356, France ceded large areas to the English and, for the first time, the English language became the daily vernacular of the law courts of London.

The 1360 Treaty of Bretigny between England and France altered English policy toward Ireland. The Irish Council, a group of powerful Anglo-Irish noblemen who controlled the Pale and policy within Ireland, persuaded Edward III to become more involved in the running of the country. He sent his second son Lionel, Earl of Ulster, to Ireland with an army of 197 men-at-arms and 670 archers, more for prestige then force. The intention was to impress the nobility of Ireland, enforce royal dominion and develop the country as a resource of men and money. His army was to be paid out of Irish revenue and, if there was no cash, by IOUs stamped with Lionel's privy seal.

By 1364, England was maintaining three armies: one in Ireland, one along the Scottish border, and another with the Black Prince in Aquitaine. Expenses in Ireland were exceeding the Irish revenue by some £6,000 sterling a year for military wages and supplies. When cash ran out, English administrators were expected to fund everything themselves and claim it back later. Lionel was the son of the king and quite a rich man who could afford such subvention, but the next justiciar, William of Windsor, saw what was coming and insisted on getting the cash (£20,000 sterling) before he left for Ireland.

Between 1361 and 1376, £91,035 sterling was spent on wages for the army in Ireland, in comparison to £634,900 sterling spent on the wars in France between 1368 and 1375. The army was in Ireland to expand the territory under English jurisdiction and it needed consistent support and finance to succeed. With the wars in France taking most of England's attention, there was no policy success in Ireland and the considerable expense of the army was wasted. [Connolly, 1981] In Leinster in particular, the MacMurroughs succeeded in recovering most of their ancient lands of Hy-Kinsella, a great stretch of fertile pasture stretching from Mount Leinster and its woods across to Ferns and further south.

The MacMurroughs, O'Tooles and O'Byrnes harassed the Anglo-Normans so much that the colony disappeared as a viable entity along the Leinster coast and, by 1372, the Dublin government offered the MacMurroughs a payment of eighty marks per annum to leave them alone. This was paid every year until 1536.

By the 1350s, families of Norman descent, such as the Harolds, Archbolds, St. Aubyns (now Tobins) and others, were seen as 'Irish', in the sense that the Dublin administration took hostages from them, as they did from the Irish, demanding that the leaders of these Gaelicised 'clans' hold themselves responsible for the behaviour of their people. The more upland and frontier-like were the lands of these families, the more they resembled their Gaelic neighbours. In 1300, Adam St. Aubyn provided for one of his sons by awarding him grazing rights and permission to cut timber and turf from the woods and bogs on their property at Cumsy, on the Tipperary-Kilkenny border. The landscape they shared with their Gaelic neighbours, the physical danger and the sense of insecurity encouraged patterns of familial relationship quite unlike those in contemporary England. [Frame, 1982]

RICHARD II AND IRELAND

The later 14th century saw an apparently amicable peace arranged between Richard II and the Irish chieftains and 'Captains' of their nation. Richard sought good personal relationships with the Irish princes if they recognised his rights as Lord of Ireland, and letters on record show that the Irish had confidence in his good faith. Niall Mór, grandson of King Domhnall O'Neill, was among the first group of Irish nobility to offer voluntary submission to Richard, asking that he 'be a shield and helmet of justice to me between my lord, the earl of Ulster and me, in case he be provoked by stern advice to exact more from me than he should.' O'Neill provoked an argument with Earl Mortimer in the king's presence during the ceremony of liege homage at Drogheda in 1395 and in a fury made the point that, while he was a vassal of the Earl of Ulster, he was nevertheless king over the lesser nobles such as O'Hanlon, MacMahon and O'Cahan, whereas Mortimer insisted that all the Ulster nobility were the same. The same income would derive to the Earl, but O'Neill's privileges and royal esteem would be less.

By May 1395, Ireland had been returned to peace for the time being. More than 80 of the most senior Irish chieftains submitted to the king, together with their tanists. It is around this time that the Irish kings 'lost' their 'king' name-tags and became MacCarthy Mór or O'Conor Don, although the MacMurroughs continued to use the title 'Rex Lagenie' on their seal up to the reign of Henry VIII.

The Great Seal of
Henry VIII.

Relations appeared good between the king and the Irish, and Gerald O'Byrne was granted a royal 'pension' of eighty marks per annum (around £60), allowing him to travel to London in style with Carragh Kavanagh, Donough O'Byrne, Thomas MacMurrough and ten other Irish nobles to consult about Ireland. It was reported in England that these Irish nobles were willing to lend support to Richard in any trouble he might have and they wore his heraldic 'badge', the White Hart, as proof of their allegiance. Another Irish chief, Taigh O'Carroll, Prince of Ely O'Carroll, felt warmly enough to call on Richard in London on his way back from Rome. Richard granted all these chiefs generous pensions and they and O'Carroll joined their royal friend for a suitably *grand* visit to Calais.

The visit of 1395 was a triumph for the Gaelic chiefs, who were now convinced of their legal status as landholders, while also being the liegemen of King Richard. Some of the Irish nobility, such as the O'Kennedys, had to acknowledge local lords like the Earl of Ormond as their overlords, but the general feeling was that a status had been achieved whereby English law and legal tenure had been established for the majority of the Irish nobility.

ULSTER

In Ulster, the 14th century saw the beginning of an attempt by many Irish chiefs, and the O'Neills of Tir Eoghan in particular, to become vassals of the king. When Brian O'Neill, chosen to be the future king of Ireland when the English were ejected, was killed at the battle of Down in 1260, he was succeeded by Hugh Buidhe as the 'Great O'Neill' who in 1269 signed a charter acknowledging that he held his lands from Walter de Burgh, Earl of Ulster. He then delivered his children to de Burgh as hostages. He married a cousin of the earl, supported de Burgh in minor wars and rendered a substantial annual tribute of cattle. The problem was that de Burgh continued to expand his lands by force, menacing the bishop and clergy of Derry to acquire part of their church lands and forcing O'Cahan to cede a large section of the woods of Glenconkeine. The Irish kings found themselves in the invidious position of being bound to de Burgh under law. This should have given them security of their ancient lands and 'kingly' rights within the territories, but in truth, the earl did what he wished and many Irish kings could get no satisfaction from their supposedly royal 'protector' in England.

Domhnall O'Neill, King of Tir Eoghan, was one of a number of Irish lords who approached John de Hothun, the royal envoy of Edward II, with letters seeking the redress of past wrongs, asking (again) to hold their lands from the monarch and requesting legal protection from rapacious officials. O'Neill requested that Edward I bring their claims before royal arbitration, but these requests were ignored, despite appealing to Pope John XXII to intervene on their behalf. When the Brown Earl of Ulster was murdered in 1333, the Inishowen peninsula was taken over by a chieftainly family called O'Dogherty, originally based in Tir Eoghan. They retained the lordship of Inishowen until the rebellion and death of Sir Cahir O'Dogherty in 1608.

By 1399, Richard was back in Ireland to remake the peace, together with a large band of royal supporters. While he was in the country, a previously banished opponent, Bolingbroke, returned to England from France. Richard hurried back but was isolated and taken to Pontefract Castle, the power base of his rivals, the Lancastrians. A group of his friends attempted to murder the usurper, Bolingbroke, but were caught. Richard was killed soon after.

Submision of Irish Chieftains, c. 1580. John Derrick engraving, courtesy the National Library of Ireland.

15TH CENTURY

This was also the era when English monarchs began to see Ireland as an increasing financial burden and to withdraw the monetary support required to anglicise the area outside the Pale and English towns. It resulted in a delegation of royal authority to the lords on the border areas, with a subsequent increase in their personal power and prestige. This created problems, in that local magnates with considerable freedom of action were required to control Ireland. These, in turn, began to see themselves as outside the jurisdiction of royal power. In addition, the three families which held that power, the Butlers, Earls of Ormond; the FitzGeralds, Earls of Kildare; and the FitzGeralds, Earls of Desmond, were becoming Gaelicised. Many of their kin had married Irish women, including Richard, brother of the Earl of Ormond, who married Catherine O'Reilly, whose family later succeeded to the title, and Richard's son, known as MacRisteard, who married Catherine O'Carroll of Ely. Another Butler, Lady Joan, married Taig O'Carroll, Lord of Ely, 'a man of great account and fame with the professors of poetry and music of Ireland and Scotland'. Unfortunately in 1417, a dispute between O'Carroll and Ormond became a small war in which O'Carroll was killed. [Curtis, 1955]

Outside the great lordships, the Gaelic and Old English families were even more intermarried and Gaelicised. The de Burgos had become Burkes and Bourkes, the Mandevilles had become MacQuillans, and most were speaking Irish as their primary language.

FURTHER POLITICAL DEVELOPMENTS

By the start of the 15th century, the great seal of Ireland, if affixed to a statute, was held by those in Ireland to be superior in law to any seal or statute in England. In Naas in 1441, the Great Council of Ireland held 'that all pleas can be heard in Irish courts'. This led to severe problems when officials arrived from England with their appointments made under the seal of England. While self-interest was the motivation for much of the opposition to English rule, by the middle of the century, leading English lawyers understood that Irish legislative independence had a certain right. The Irish parliament of 1460 declared that 'the land of Ireland ... corporate of itself by [its] ancient laws and customs ... is freed of the burden of any special law of the realm of England ... save only such laws ... admitted and accepted ... [by Ireland].' Irish separatism was enjoying a false spring.

In 1460, the FitzGeralds of Kildare supported a curious individual called Lambert Simnel, who claimed to be the rightful heir to the throne of England. They were Yorkists, and that year they had supported the Duke of York in his bid for the throne. They were also involved in a later pretender, Perkin Warbeck, who landed at Cork in 1491. During this period, the earls of Kildare had manipulated Henry VI and Richard III and had obtained increases in salary, resisting appointments of those they did not like and generally working the system to their benefit. The Kildares were supposed to support their monarch, but in 1487 and again in 1491/92, the eighth earl failed to support the king when he should have done so.

In 1495, the number of English troops in Ireland was calculated at 330, plus 100 Irish kerne, probably the Keatings. In some ways this seems a tiny 'army' if conquest was the aim, and the cost, £3,829 per annum, was modest. Parliaments were held at Dublin and Drogheda to raise this amount because the king wished Ireland to be self-supporting in defence terms against the Irish outside the English-controlled areas. A tax was raised by levying two marks, about euro 12,500 in todays money, per ploughland inside the Pale and one mark per ploughland outside, raising over £1,503 for the year 1495/96. The difference was that, instead of being a 'once-off' levy, this was to continue for five years, forming an ongoing tax, 'without which' the Dublin administration noted, 'the land may not be defended'. Those paying the tax had a legitimate self-interest in being protected.

ARISTOCRATIC HOME RULE

By the late 15th century, Ireland had a type of Home Rule, under the FitzGeralds, earls of Kildare. But a new deputy, Sir Edward Poynings, introduced a policy out that would spell division in the present and war in the future. He called a parliament in Drogheda in 1494 and forced through an act that 'all laws passed in England shall be valid for Ireland', meaning that all laws, even those passed centuries previously, would be legal in Ireland. The further stipulation was that the somewhat independent Dublin parliament could not enact any law for Ireland without it being approved in England first. Poynings' Law ended Ireland's legislative autonomy. Thereafter, the Tudors tightened the reins on the fiefdoms within the country and ultimately destroyed the powerful and independent FitzGeralds of Kildare and Desmond, and their subsidiary Irish lords. Initially however, Henry VIII's most important policy was 'Surrender and Regrant' which was a diplomatic masterpiece. For little cost, many of the greatest Irish chieftains surrendered their independence in return for what was promised as individual ownership of their territories and an Irish title. But it set members of the great families against one another; it diminished their families' sovereignty and made them, ultimately, dependent on the crown.

Henry's daughter, Elizabeth I, continued the policy of conquest and reformation and ultimately confiscated about three million acres from their ancient owners. In the 16th century, England was aware that Ireland could be a foothold for Spain or France and was determined that it should not be so. Equally, commercial envy was a motivation in policy. Guerau de Spes, a Spanish diplomat in London, wrote in 1570: 'England keeps Ireland poor so as to make the island unattractive to a foreign prince, and they have no wish to civilise it because they think it might become more populous and powerful than this island'. [Spanish State Papers 1569-1579, quoted in Maxwell, 1923]

IRISH PARLIAMENTS

Parliaments were the 'Great Councils' whereby the king and his archbishops, bishops and barons could meet and discuss what the king wanted to do. There was no representation for ordinary people in any parliament until the 19th century.

The first recorded parliament in Ireland was in 1264 and by the end of that century, as in England, representatives from the new shires, liberties and towns attended. Particular parliaments were called for specific reasons. For example, in 1366, the Statutes of Kilkenny were called into being by Lionel of Clarence to prevent closer integration of Norman and Irish, forbidding the wearing of Irish clothes and use of the language. The 1460 parliament at Drogheda declared Ireland independent of England in a bid by Richard, Duke of York to gain the English crown from an Irish base. Poynings' Parliament of 1494 was an attempt to reduce the power of the Anglo-Irish lords by making sure that an Irish parliament could meet only with royal permission and with approval of the laws to be enacted. It was 1536 before the Gaelic Irish lords were admitted to an Irish parliament.

Irish parliaments met in 1536 and 1537 to ratify the Reformation and sort out the distribution of monastic lands, and further parliaments were called for 1541 and 1543 to establish Ireland as a kingdom. The 1543 parliament, under Sir Thomas Cusack, Sheriff of Meath, debated the policy of Surrender and Regrant which guaranteed the

Gaelic Irish secure title to their lands. It was deemed by all to be a great success and was the first to be well attended by the Gaelic nobility, including the Upper MacWilliam (Burke) and the Lower MacWilliam (Bourke), O'Connor Roe and O'Connor Sligo. It was at this parliament that Upper MacWilliam surrendered his ancient Irish title and was created Earl of Clanrickard. Sir Anthony St. Leger wrote a report of the parliament to Henry VIII, mentioning that the proceedings were conducted in 'the Irish tongue', translated by the Earl of Ormond and that when it was declared (in Irish) that Henry VIII should be from henceforth the King of Ireland, 'the whole house most willingly and joyously consented and agreed'. Following this successful parliament, the Anglo-Irish and Gaelic Lords attended a 'sung solemn mass' in St. Patrick's and, afterwards, the act was proclaimed in the presence of over 2,000 notables of the country, with a Te Deum sung 'with great joy and gladness' in thanksgiving. In theological terms, it was not until 1551 that the Book of Common Prayer was introduced to replace the missal, and the Reformation assumed a new, liturgical role in the worship of the people.

Interestingly, although the Gaels and the *Anglais* of Ireland celebrated Mass on Corpus Christi and other Holy Days, and while Henry himself was a practising Catholic, the king's deputy in Ireland, St. Leger mentions in his reports the continuing 'extirpation of the power of the Bishop of Rome who hath been...a great robber and destroyer of this your realm'. He established a commission established in 1539 to 'enquire as to the whereabouts of notable images or relics at which the simple people were wont to superstitiously meet together'. When found, they were to be broken or carried away. The Reforming administration carried out an enormous amount of demolition, including the burning of the statue of the Blessed Virgin of Trim and the Bacall Íosa (staff of Jesus) in Dublin. The Annals of the Four Masters mentions the depredations and demolitions as the roofs and bells of the monasteries and friaries were sold and the farmlands broken up. This had another effect, because the monastic lands were the best managed and most productive in the country, and those who

acquired the lands had neither the manpower nor the knowledge to continue working the lands as before.

A medieval parliament showing King, nobles and clergy.

Further parliaments met to reintroduce Catholicism during the reign of Queen Mary (1555-58) and to establish Anglicanism (1560). The Desmond rebellions tainted the atmosphere of the following years and in 1584, when Elizabeth I appointed Sir John Perrot to bring the Irish to good order after the war in Munster, there had been no parliament for six years. He arrived in Dublin on 21 June, accompanied by Sir Thomas Norrys, who was to be president of Munster, and Sir Richard Bingham as president of Connacht. Perrot went on a circuit of the country to find out for himself the state of things and arrived in Dublin that winter. In spring of the following year, he summoned a parliament in Dublin with probably the greatest number of Gaelic representatives to attend any such event.

Irish Attendees for the Dublin Parliament of 1585

Turlough Luineach (The) O'Neill,

Hugh O'Neill, Baron of Dungannon,

Hugh O'Donnell, Lord of Tyrconnell,

Cuconnaght Maguire, Lord of Fermanagh

John Oge O'Doherty, Lord of Inishowen,

Turlough O'Boyle, Lord of Boylagh of Donegal,

Owen O'Gallagher, Marshal to O'Donnell,

Ross MacMahon, Chief of Oriel,

Rory O'Kane, Lord of Oireacht-O'Cahane,

Con O'Neill, Lord of Clannaboy,

Shane McBrien O'Neill, Knight for the County
    of Antrim,

Hugh Magennis, Lord of Iveagh,

Sir Brian O'Rourke,

John Roe O'Reilly and Edmond O'Reilly, Knights
    for the County Cavan,

O'Farrell Ban and O'Farrell Buidhe, Knights
    for the County Longford,

Hugh, son of the O'Conor Don

Teige Oge O'Conor Roe,

Donnell O'Connor-Sligo,

Brian MacDermot, Deputy of the MacDermot
    of Moylurg,

Carbry O'Brien, Lord of Tir-Bruin-na-Sinna in
    Roscommon,

Teigh O'Kelly of Mullaghmore,

Donal O'Madden,

Ulick Burke, Earl of Clanrickard,

John and Dermot O'Shaughnessy,

Murrough-of-the-Battle-Axes-O'Flaherty,

Donough O'Brien, Earl of Thomond,

Sir Tirlough O'Brien, Knight of the County
    Clare,

Turlough, son of Teige O'Brien,

John MacNamara,

Rossa O'Loughlin of the Burren,

Boetius O'Clancy, Brehon of Thomond and
    Knight of County Clare,

Mac-i-Brien Ara, Protestant Bishop of Killaloe
    and Chief of his name,

Calvagh O'Carroll,

John MacCoghlan,

Philip O'Dwyer of Kilnamanagh in Tipperary,

MacBrien of Coonagh in Limerick,

Brian dubh O'Brien, Lord of Carraiggunnell,

Conor O'Mulryan, Chief of the Two-Owneys,

Donnall MacCarthy Mor, Earl of Clancare,

Sir Owen MacCarthy Reagh of Carbery,

Dermot and Donough MacCarthy of Duhallow,

Owen O'Sullivan Beare and Owen O'Sullivan
    More,

Conor O'Mahony of Carbery,

Sir Fineen O'Driscoll More

Fineen MacGillapatrick, Lord of Upper Ossory,

Conla MacGeoghehan of Kineleagh,

Connel O'Molloy of the Kings County,

Fiach McHugh O'Byrne, Chief of Gaval-
    Rannell.

The list on the left shows the willingness of the Irish lords to acknowledge royal authority although the purpose of this parliament was to punish those who had been involved in the recent Munster rebellion, and to pass Acts of Attainder on both James, Viscount Baltinglass and the Earl of Desmond, and to confiscate their estates. In Desmond's case, the land, including that of his followers, was in excess of 574,000 acres.

EUROPEAN INVOLVEMENT
SPAIN

James son of Maurice FitzGerald, was the first to link Catholicism with resistance to the Dublin government, thereby causing great difficulties for the Old English who wanted to remain Catholic but loyal. By combining catholicism and rebellion, FitzMaurice (FitzGerald) pushed them unwillingly into the rebel camp and intrigued with the Pope and the King of Spain to bring Ireland under Spanish rule. Philip of Spain was reluctant to enter the Irish arena and some Spanish noblemen were dismissive of the country and its people as 'beggarly, great traitors to one another and no force' [Duke de Faria, quoted in Black, 1936] Eventually a Spanish force of 600 arrived at Smerwick in County Kerry. They were besieged by Admiral Winter from the sea and Lord Grey on the land. 600 surrendered without conditions and, except for those worth ransom money, were put to the sword, as well as some Irish who had joined them.

THE REFORMATION

Although the Reformation could be said to have started officially in Ireland in 1536, when the Dublin parliament accepted Henry VIII as 'the only supreme head on earth of the whole Church of Ireland', its development into a more Lutheran orthodoxy took decades longer. Henry was not that concerned with doctrine and was focussed on authority. His experience with the Catholic faction in England and

The South Range of
Dublin Castle, first built
in the 13th century. with the FitzGeralds of Kildare, where they called on the
Pope for support, strengthened his decision to be head of the
church as well as king. His reformation policy, therefore, was
entangled with political schemes to bring the greater Irish princes
and chiefs within the control of his monarchy. On this point he was
conciliatory, changing the approach of his administrative officials to
one of friendly agreement with Irish lords, preferring them to be
obedient vassals with secure (royal) tenure rather than 'rebel Irish'.

There was no reason at first glance why clergy could not conform to the principles set out while continuing in the old traditional
liturgy and beliefs. Only the position of the Pope had changed.
Henry was styled 'King of England, Ireland and France, Defender of
the Faith, and on earth, Supreme Head of the Church of England
and Ireland'. No doctrinal changes were made to the form of the

Mass, and grants of monastic lands were extended to the chieftains. The heads of the religious orders were awarded pensions, derived from the rentals of the former monastic lands.

But apart from doctrinal matters, the medieval Catholic Church was not in good shape It had suffered as the rest of the country through civil unrest, and the Church properties were in need of repair. In areas outside government control, the position worsened. The results of the Reformation were to close down some 400 religious establishments – although the figure is misleading. Of that number, perhaps between 10 to 15 per cent were actually functioning, while tens of thousands of acres were held by monasteries with only two or three monks who leased the land to their relatives. Although there was destruction of property, in general there was little objection, as the devoutly Catholic middle-classes of the time bought and sold the land as eagerly as any government official.

As the Catholic church 'moved out', Gaelic and Norman lords took over the benefices and granges together with the income due from the great monastic estates, rendering the management and maintenance of the 'new' Church a financial burden, without any popular support. In Clonfert, the bishop's income declined from one hundred pounds in 1584 to twenty-four pounds by 1615.

A parliament was held in 1560 to reaffirm the provisions of the Reformation parliament of 1536 and added an 'Act of Uniformity', forcing attendance at Reformed Churches on Sundays on penalty of a fine. Further measures were introduced to force compliance and the persecution of friars and monks began. Between 1570 and 1603, 76 identifiable individuals, including seven Cistercians and 36 Franciscans, were executed for their religious beliefs and 20 died in miserable conditions in prison.

Henry had established a Catholic church without the Pope and many of the bishops were induced to accept the oath. Mass continued as before, except that the abbeys and friaries were wrecked and many were pulled down. This was a major blow to the very fabric of Irish society because the monasteries were the social, educational

The church of Gowran Co.Kilkenny holds the tomb of Theobald and Edward MacRichard Butler, illegitimate sons of James MacRichard Butler, both of whom died between 1337 and 1341. For Irish and Anglo-Irish alike, prowess in war, reflected effigy in death.

and 'community centres' of medieval life, especially in the countryside where Gaelic society was strongest. In addition to the cultural impact of the Reformation, Lord Leonard Grey, who had successfully negotiated the submission of O'Regan, O'Dwyer, MacCarthy Reagh and others, was recalled and executed for his lack of ruthlessness and his trust in the Irish.

Ireland remained the only country in Europe that had defied its sovereign and had remained largely Catholic. In spite of the efforts of the Dublin administration and Elizabeth's government, the Catholic Church shook but stayed fast. Rome's decision to send Jesuits to Ireland in 1541, in case Ireland should be lost to the Faith as well as to England, was the spur for the Counter-Reformation on the island. [Curtis, 1955]

Ireland was seen as a threat to England so long as her people adhered to the Church of Rome and were only loosely attached to the English crown. The Protestantisation of Ireland must have appeared as much a necessity for England's defence as for Ireland's salvation. In addition, the Anglican Church, with the monarch at its head, automatically inculcated obedience to that power and condemned any act of disobedience to the civil authorities. The attempt to make Ireland Protestant by military enactment proved futile and even the Dublin parliament, normally supine to England's wishes, dissolved itself on 11 January 1560 'by reason of its aversion to the Protestant religion'. [Maxwell, 1923]

The Catholic Church retained a diocesan system and, where it was politically unwise to appoint a bishop, priests were designated as Vicar Apostolic, with the power of a bishop. Efforts continued to fine recusants (those who refused to attend the services of the Reformed church) and a sum of one shilling per Sunday absence was levied but rarely collected on those who retained the 'old faith'.

Perhaps one important difference in the success of the Reformation in England and its failure in Ireland was related to education. In England, the reformed faith was taught through the

educational system, while in Ireland no such *system* existed. The schools that survived the destruction of the monasteries had large numbers of students, were Catholic and ensured a continuity of faith and a supply of vocations. The Reformation began to falter in its unsteady progress by the beginning of the 17th century from a lack of diocesan funds, little support from government, low parish numbers and general disillusionment. By 1628, a Cambridge-educated Kilkenny Protestant, William Daniel, while Archbishop of Tuam, was reported have 'taken to drink, tobacco and the bed'.

The incoming Elizabethan reformers were dismissive of native clergy, and Yorkshire-born Adam Loftus, Archbishop of Armagh 1562-67 and Archbishop of Dublin 1567-1605, characterised John Garvey, the Irish-speaking bishop who succeeded him in Armagh as 'no preacher, and inclined to papistry, if he have any religion at all'. Despite the reforming zeal of its promoters, Protestantism was viewed with distaste, and outside the cities, many Anglican clergy returned to their faith of baptism. By 1605, the lack of Irish rectors and the growing numbers of ordinands from England emphasised the difference between the groups on the island, and Protestantism became identified solely with the English state.

The policy attempted by Loftus was to use financial coercion (recusancy fines) as a means to theological conversion. It failed because of the resistance of the people and the willingness of the Catholic merchant and landed class to pay the fines and go to jail if necessary, rather than attend Morning Service. By the 1620s, English policy, as dictated to the Church of Ireland, was that Catholicism was to be tolerated, if not officially approved.

Having exterminated the Kildare Geraldines, Henry VIII returned to his policy of 'sober ways, politic drifts and amiable persuasions'. He distributed monastic lands to favourites for small sums and that guaranteed their loyalty, as in England. In 1540 Henry was declared King of Ireland, but this title went beyond his person and all subsequent kings of England were also kings of Ireland. The unfortunate result of this policy was that the Irish loyally followed James

The 15th century-King's Castle in Kilmallock, Co. Limerick, once the magnificent walled town of the FitzGeralds of Desmond, with many stone houses, churches and other buildings. It was largely destroyed in 1570 by Sir James FitzMaurice Fitzgerald captain of the Desmond forces, with help from the Sweeneys and Sheehys, 'so that it became an abode of wolves'. [Killanin, 1962]

II after the English parliament deprived him of his throne in 1689. To the Irish nobility, Gaelic and Old English alike, James was their rightful king in law and in religion. The majority of the Dublin parliament that had declared Henry VIII King of Ireland was English by birth or descent, and the Earl of Desmond, Lord Barry, Lord Roche and other Munster lords attended, while O'Brien of Thomond was represented. Irish chieftains who came in person included MacGillapatrick of Upper Ossory. The Chancellor's speech declaring Henry's kingship was translated into Irish for the Gaelic and Norman (now Old English) nobility because they had little English. [Curtis, 1955] Henry's policy, however, was to turn Ireland into another

The Great Seal of Queen Elizabeth I affixed to documents to render them legal

England and there was no place for the Irish language, or for Irish customs or traditions in that plan.

The Catholic Church had, over the centuries, become more than a religious institution in Ireland. By the late Middle Ages, it was part of an elaborate social structure of land tenure, inheritance and patronage of the arts. The effect of the Reformation was to destroy this essential structure of Gaelic life. New laws were passed forbidding intermarriage and fostering children with the Irish. No Irish minstrels, bards or rhymers were to be permitted in English lands. By an act against absentees, claims on land from the original Norman conquest were revived, adding to the vast amount of land available for 'redistribution'.

In 1534, Connor O'Brien, styling himself 'Prince of Ireland', wrote to the Holy Roman Emperor Charles V, seeking help. He states plainly in the letter, 'Ever since that time [the conquest] we have not ceased to oppose the English intruders ... we have never been subject to English rule, or yielded up our ancient liberties ... we will serve your Majesty with all our force, with 1,600 horse and 2,440 foot, equipped and armed, and will levy [an additional] 13,000 men, armed with harquebus, bows, arrows and swords ... at your majesty's disposition, to be employed as you direct.' The Council of Ireland met on 18 January 1540 and discussed the 'detestable traitors', FitzGerald, O'Neill, O'Donnell, the Earl of Desmond, Connor O'Brien, O'Connor, and O'Mulloy. So displeased was the Council with their 'tyrannous purposes', among which was their wish to reassert the primacy of the Pope, that 'extreme punishment' was recommended for these leaders. The same Council considered 'the whole extirpation and total destruction of all the Irishmen of the land', but the idea was shelved because of the cost and difficulty. [Maxwell, 1923]

In Connacht, English authority was slowly overtaking the old ways. In 1537, Sir Leonard Grey received a submission from The Upper MacWilliam (Burke), The O'Flaherty, The O'Madden and other chieftains. After their ennoblement in 1543, the Clanrickard Burkes acted as a royal authority in Connacht, especially over the suspected involvement of the Mayo Bourkes with O'Neill. In 1558, Tibbot-ne-Long Bourke's father, Richard-an-Iarainn, brought in 1,200 Scots mercenaries to plunder the territories of MacMaurice and Lord Athenry. They were defeated and Richard had to escape to Mayo, beyond the Clanrickards' jurisdiction. By 1592, the Bourkes of Mayo had negotiated a submission with Sir Conyers Clifford that promised security of tenure and rights and privileges, allowing them considerable freedom as long as certain good conduct, loyalty and rent for the land was paid. Among those who submitted were Miles Bourke, Davy Bourke, the Devil's Hook (Burke), Edmond O'Malley, George McDonnell-Mac-An-Abb, Chief of Clandonnell, Walter McDonnell, Hugh Boy McDonnell, William Bourke, Brian McThomas Reagh, Walter McJordan, Thomas na Coghill, the Clandonnells of Castlelee, the Sleight Markys and the Clan Jordans. The Burkes of Galway and Bourkes of Mayo appear to have recognised a reality in their dealings with the Crown. It was preferable to use their ability and their ambition to surpass their rivals and agree to a royal tenure than to gain an illusory freedom through internal repression and constant war. [Chambers, 1983]

In 1519, Garret Óg FitzGerald, Earl of Kildare and Lord Deputy of Ireland, was called to London to answer accusations that he was intriguing with his Gaelicised kinsmen, the Earls of Desmond and the King of France. Despite presenting a plausable argument to Cardinal Wolsey, Henry VIII's advisor, the King appointed an English lord lieutenant, the first since 1460, to administer Ireland. Henry penned a memo that year to 'devise how Ireland may be reduced and restored to good order and obedience'. He further stated, in a famous despatch to the new Lord Lieutenant, Thomas Howard, that in order to bring the King's dominion to submission, it must be 'by sober ways, rather than rigorous dealings ... or any other enforcement by strength or violence ... the King expects to get back lands which he has lost, he does not wish to oppose injustice by injustice'. The despatch further assured the Irish nobility of Henry's intentions not to 'take from them that which rightly appertains to them', and Howard, as Earl of Surrey, entered into a round of meetings and agreements with O'Neill and O'Donnell, forced submissions from O'Carroll, O'More and O'Connor of Offaly, and made positive contact with the Earl of Desmond, MacCarthy Mór and MacCarthy Reagh.

In Surrey's time as deputy in Ireland, the cost of administering the colony began to be a serious topic in the king's council and Surrey put forward the idea that a complete conquest would require a different policy than conciliation and occasional military forays. He suggested that to totally defeat the Irish would take an army of 5,000 men and finance from the English exchequer to build castles, towns and bring in settlers, 'to set the Irish to labour on the land'. This idea of 'colonisation' through imported people was to inform future policy in Ireland for generations to come.

In Connacht in 1586, the new president, Sir Richard Bingham, began his tenure with such brutality that he seems to have been bordering on the psychopathic. His cruelty provoked the Burkes into rebellion, the whole point of his strategy, and Bingham hanged and murdered anyone who was remotely connected to them, even those who considered themselves under the government's protection. Bingham caught up with the Burkes' mercenary gallowglass, the MacDonnells, at Ardnaree on the Moy in September 1586 and, according to a witness, Captain Thomas Woodhouse, 'and there, God be thanked, we did drown and kill, as we all did judge, about the number of a thousand or eleven hundred ... but truly I was, never since becoming a man of war, so weary with the killing of men, for I protest to God, as fast as I could, I did hough [stab] them and paunch them, sometimes on horseback, sometimes on foot ... so in the space of a hour, this whole and good field was done'. [Maxwell, 1923]

The Gathering Storm

CHAPTER

8

T HE 16TH CENTURY was when much of what could have been Irish, in the sense of a 'nation' coming into being, was lost. Both the Irish and Old English made choices in the wars that accompanied and followed the Reformation, and both found themselves outmanoeuvred and on the losing side. It was the era when political change became state policy, with a punitive regime, rather than individual negotiation between monarch and 'great subject' or 'Irish rebel'. There would be no more token submissions and payment of fines. The Irish and Old English lords lost their personal wars in the 16th century and, unwittingly, lost them for Ireland.

It was the time when confiscation and colonisation became policy against Irish and Old English alike. The vast bulk of the land of Ireland changed hands between about 1560 and 1660 and left most of the Gaelic and Catholic inhabitants landless in their own country.

What remained was the enormous range of medieval buildings created to house, educate and spiritually sustain the Gaelic and Old English families that were the ruling classes of the time. The richly endowed monasteries and abbeys showed the skills of Irish stonecutters and the secular and spiritual gifts of their benefactors and residents. The same period saw the Gaelic tongue decline from being the cultivated language of landowners and lawyers to the earthy mutterings of tenant farmers and angry poets.

Coppinger's Court was built by a member of that family in the early years of the 17th century. The Coppingers' supplied sixteen mayors of Cork and Youghal between 1558 and 1625 and were 'Old English' merchants in Munster since the early middle-ages. [Brady & Gillespie, 1986]

Dunluce Castle, Co.
Antrim, seat of the
MacDonnell family who
helped many of the
Spanish ship-wrecked in
the Armada off 1588 to
escape to Scotland.

It was during the 16th century that religion coloured the conflicts within Ireland. Both the 9 years war and the Desmond rebellion were, amongst other things, Catholic revolts against a Protestant state.

Elizabeth I came to power in 1558. She had been reared a Protestant, but had attended Mass during the previous reign of her sister. She was lucky to be there at all. Her father, Henry VIII, had executed her mother and she was nearly executed by her sister, Mary, who had succeeded him. When it came to religion, Elizabeth was a liberal of those terrible times and called herself 'Governor of the Church', rather than 'Head of the Church', trying to establish a religion that was in between old-style Catholicism and the new Anglicanism. Compromise seemed a way forward and most people

in England seemed to accept the 'new' Church of England. In 1570 the Pope, however, excommunicated Elizabeth, declared her parents to have never been married and released all her subjects in Ireland and England from obedience to her. This forced a change of mood. Catholics were now perceived as possible traitors and over 200 were executed between the Pope's declaration and the collapse of the Spanish invasion threat and the Armada in 1588.

15th-century oak carvings on the choir seats [misericords] of St Mary's Cathedral, Limerick.

FALL OF THE HOUSE OF KILDARE

In the Middle Ages, where Capel Street and Mary Street in Dublin now stand was the largest and richest monastery in Ireland, its spires and cloisters surrounded by monks' dormitories and domestic buildings. The farm lands of St Mary's Abbey are now underneath Dublin's fruit and vegetable market. Under the surrounding streets are the remnants of the tiled floors and stone foundations of that abbey, the pride of the Irish Cistercians. But it provided something else in addition to religious life. In a modern sense, it housed conference facilities, supplying accommodation and a meeting room, the Chapter House, for the Great Council of Ireland, a precursor of the cabinet that ran the country on behalf of the Crown.

Since the middle of the 15th century, the FitzGerald earls of Kildare had dominated that council and defeated all attempts to remove them in favour of more compliant officials. The 8th Earl, Garret Mór (1456-1513) was the dominant figure in Irish politics for almost 30 years, serving under five kings of England and managing the complex set of relationships between the Crown, the Irish and the 'Old English', the descendants of the Normans. The FitzGeralds were related to many of the leading Gaelic families and Garret Óg (1487-1534), who succeeded his father, married his daughter to Brian O'Connor-Faly, a neighbouring chieftain. He never attained the greatness of his father and was frequently detained in London while being accused by his enemies of 'seditious practices, conspiracies and subtill draftes'. In 1532, Garret Óg was appointed deputy for the last time for the last time and in 1534 he was called to London and imprisoned for allegedly using the king's artillery for his own defence. [MacCurtain, 1972]

On 11 June 1534, the Great Council of Ireland met in the Chapter House of Mary's Abbey. Garret Óg was in the Tower and had left his son, Silken Thomas, Lord Offaly, in charge. Rumours were about that Garret had been executed and that the FitzGeralds were to be removed as deputies, losing the considerable revenue and prestige which they considered their own and no one else's. They were also known to be opposed to the Reformation which was gathering pace in England at this time.

Around 3 o'clock, the council were alarmed to see 140 horsemen gallop up, wearing the red and white silk of the FitzGeralds, and led by 22-year-old Silken Thomas. He was enraged, believing his father to be dead and the Kildare power under threat. Thomas held the Sword of Office as Royal Deputy, the 'governor' of Ireland in the king's absence and, to the horror of the assembled officials, he flung down the sword and declared himself the enemy of Henry VIII. He had entered this room as a rich young peer of the realm, the king's governor in Ireland, but he left it as a rebel. He would be dead before he was 24.

Many reasons have been put forward as to why Thomas behaved in such a way. It had been FitzGerald tactics before to orchestrate upheaval around the Pale when Garret Mor or Garret Og were recalled to London for a reprimand, thereby showing that an earl of Kildare and only an earl of Kildare was capable of keeping order on the marches. However, closer examination of Thomas's strategy suggests that it was a wider appeal to others to actually rebel against the king as a heretic that motivated Thomas and not just a token rattling of swords to ensure his family's continuation in power.

MAYNOOTH CASTLE

This sad rebellion came to an abrupt end at Maynooth Castle. This was the main seat of the FitzGeralds, with its own college, founded by the family in 1521. The castle was originally built c.1203 by Gerald FitzMaurice, 1st Baron Offaly and ancestor of the earls of Kildare, and was enlarged in 1426 by the 6th Earl. The 8th and 9th Earls, Garret Mór and Garret Óg had a notable library of manuscripts and printed books of Irish, Latin, French and English literature. As the main castle of the earls of Kildare, the interior was described as having beautiful wall hangings, fine furniture, gold candlesticks and a resident Ollamh (Philosopher/Historian) Paidin O'Mulcrony, a Gaelic-speaking tutor for the Geraldine children.

Silken Thomas was supported in his rebellion by O'Neill, O'More, MacMurrough, O'Connor-Faly and O'Byrne, but failed to take Dublin and, despite seeking help from abroad, his rebellion began to fail. He had hoped to join his kinsmen, the FitzGeralds of Desmond, in an alliance with the emperor Charles V and certainly used the Catholic cause as a rallying point. But his ambassador,

The Tower of London in the 15th century, used to house important prisioners.

Charles Reynolds, Archdeacon of Kells, returned from the Pope and the emperor with no troops to fight against England. His father died in the Tower in December 1534, apparently when he heard that his son had gone into rebellion. [McCorristine, 1987]

Maynooth Castle became the hiding place for his frightened supporters and was attacked by Skeffington, the ruthless deputy sent over to defeat the rebellion. It was bombarded for seven days until a breach

was made in the walls. The constable of the castle, Christopher Parrish, arranged a parley and was offered cash and the promise of life for the remaining 60 members of the garrison if they surrendered. They did, but Skeffington reneged on the deal, hanging 30 and beheading 25. He skewered their heads on the burnt towers of the castle as 'a warning to others'. The pardon of Maynooth became an ironic term for all subsequent breaches of trust.

Eventually Silken Thomas's five FitzGerald uncles surrendered on a promise of pardon and were taken by ship to England and the Tower of London. An ancient prophecy had foretold the ruin of the House of Kildare if five sons of an earl travelled to England in the belly of a cow. The ship was called *The Cow*. They knew that the

Romanesque heads from the doorcase of Dysert O'Dea church, Co. Clare.

prophecy would be fulfilled. And on 3 February 1537, one by one, Silken Thomas and his five uncles were hanged, drawn and quartered at Tyburn. Ireland's aristocratic home rule was over. [MacGeoghegan,1844]

THE DESMOND REBELLIONS (1569-73 and 1579-83)

The FitzGeralds of Desmond were the foremost family in Munster for most of the medieval period. They had arrived as Normans, but by the early 14th century were Gaelic speaking while, nominally at least, representing royal authority in Munster. The Irish poets praised Maurice, the 1st Earl (created 1329), who had fought against Edward Bruce in Ireland, was imprisoned from 1331 to 1333 and outlawed from 1334 to 1339, as 'kingworthy'. The 3rd Earl, Gerald, was a poet in Gaelic and wrote several poems about his captivity under Conor O'Brien from 1370 to 1371.

By 1416, the FitzGeralds of Askeaton had an O'Daly as a resident poet in the castle and their interest in education showed in their establishment of a college in Youghal in 1462. The founder of that college, Thomas, the 8th Earl of Desmond, was appointed Lord Deputy of Ireland in 1463 and began a close co-operation with his kinsman, the Earl of Kildare. He attempted to establish a university at Drogheda in 1465 so that those Irishmen who were shut out of Oxford might learn the law. The new deputy, Tiptoft, Earl of Worcester, arrested the earls of Desmond and of Kildare and Edward Plunkett, the sheriff of Meath. The Earl of Desmond was executed without trial, causing uproar throughout Munster and a serious loss of faith in the rule of English law among the 'Old English' in Ireland. Following this judicial murder, the Desmonds withdrew from participation in Dublin government and turned towards Munster for their inspiration. After his death, Desmond's daughter Catherine married MacCarthy Reagh and commissioned the Book of Lismore, compiled from the remnants of the (now) lost book of Monasterboice. [Stopford-Greene, 1908]

THE FALL OF THE HOUSE OF DESMOND

The earls of Desmond, although Norman in origin, had become gaelicised over time, but their independence and that of their vassals was paramount, and they were unwilling to compromise feudal authority to any monarch or parliament of England or Ireland. They found the imposition of sheriffs and officials a threat and an insult – and a curbing of their power. It was of course, a trap by the Dublin administration, just as their London counterparts incited, provoked and then executed great lords in the same century.

From today's viewpoint, Garret FitzGerald seems foolhardy, rash and with a tongue suited to the stage rather than politics, but he was a figure of some stature in that period and appeared to many as someone who might just recover the independence and old ways of feudal Munster. That territory was always a prosperous province and had several important cities and an overseas trade for its timber, hides and wool. It had roads, bridges and monasteries that provided the basics of education and, in some cases, administration for the greater lords.

In 1573, Askeaton was the stage from which the Earl of Desmond, one of the last great Gaelic lords, began the journey to his unfortunate and cruel destiny. He was, like his contemporaries, out of touch to a great degree with the lengths to which his Elizabethan opponents were prepared to go to steal his land and his great inheritance. He was no leader, no warrior, and his appearance before the cheering crowds at Askeaton, while appearing like the resurrection of their hopes of freedom of a sort, merely heralded further destruction. He was an 'antique' in many ways, a feudal ruler of the largest private territory in Ireland or England, but through circumstances and personality, he was unsuited to the job. His enemies – and as a great lord he had many – saw his weakness and took advantage. His irresponsible and sometimes bizarre behaviour led his opponents to believe they could take his land and his wealth. They did. The story of the destruction of Desmond is well documented through the efforts of historian Anne Chambers who chronicles so accurately the

An English army with heads of the slain Irish c. 1580. John Derrick engraving, courtesy the National Library of Ireland.

decline and fall of both a dynasty and a way of life for those whose fortunes were allied with the family. In many ways the story of the FitzGeralds of Desmond was not unique. Gaelic aristocrats had been cheated, murdered, deprived in every way possible of what was rightfully theirs, and Chambers chronicles in detail how such things were accomplished.

His appearance at Askeaton was a last hurrah for Munster, as he refused to adapt and reduce his great power in the face of Elizabeth's requests. He unwittingly moved from being a magnate intent on recovering all his sequestered territory, to being a rebel with Spanish help that might threaten the realm of England. Garret was unsuited to manage such a venture, but that did not prevent thousands of Munster soldiers and swordsmen from flocking to Askeaton to join his cause and roar 'Shanid Abú', (Up Shanid!), the war cry of the FitzGeralds. By not recognising the new political reality of Elizabethan England, Garret and his like condemned Gaelic Ireland to oblivion.

The Pope became involved, confirming English suspicions about Irish loyalty, and Gregory XIII granted jurisdiction over Limerick to the Earl of Desmond in May 1580. The Earl appealed to his countrymen 'to join in the defence of our Catholic faith against the Englishmen which have overrun our country'. [MacCurtain, 1972] Many did and Fiach McHugh O'Byrne rose in rebellion, as did Lord Baltinglass. A force of Spaniards under Colonel San Joseph landed at Smerwick in Kerry and, after some inconsequential manoeuvres, surrendered unconditionally to a force under Captains Mackworth, Raleigh and Zouche. All 600 excepting San Joseph were massacred. This disaster and its cruel nature sent a message to others. Baltinglass fled and Fiach O'Byrne sued for terms of surrender. The English gradually took control of Youghal, Carrigofoyle and Askeaton Castle, and captured James, the Earl of Desmond's younger and smarter brother. He was hanged and quartered in Cork and his head stuck on a spike on the North Gate for three months.

The wars in Munster reduced the most prosperous part of the island to ruin and famine and the reprisals against the rebels were harsh, even by Elizabethan standards. Sir John Perrot, President of Munster from 1571, executed 800 people within two years of his appointment. A scorched earth policy was used to force the rebels into submission and Sir William Drury, Lord President of Munster, commented, 'I give the rebels no breath to relieve themselves ... they be continually hunted, I keep them from their harvest and have taken great preys [herds] of cattle from them ... the poor people offer their wives and children to be slain by the army rather than suffer the famine which is upon them.'

This sad and wilful destruction of Munster was alleviated only when the Earl of Desmond was murdered by the Moriartys on 11 November 1583. His head was sent to London as a trophy of victory and over 500,000 acres were confiscated, with estates varying from 2,000 to 12,000 acres parcelled out to those who had goaded and provoked the FitzGeralds into war and those who wished to settle in Ireland. The attainted wealth of one 'rebel', John FitzEdmund of

Cloyne, amounted to £6,157 sterling and Sir Owen MacCarthy's income was calculated at £2,500 sterling per annum for the years 1569-73. This was a time when a landed gentleman of England was considered well off with £1,750 sterling a year. It was the wealth of Munster that was wanted. Walter Raleigh, one of the people who had orchestrated the acts that caused the rebellion and who had also served at Smerwick as a Captain of Foot, was especially rewarded with 42,000 acres between Youghal and Lismore. The rents were cheap. Edward Denny and his heirs had to pay £50 for 6,000 acres of County Kerry. In total, from 202,099 acres, the crown received rents of £1,967 sterling. [Connolly, 1998]

By 1599, Munster was recovering from the devastation of the Desmond rebellion. It had the greatest numbers of walled towns of the four provinces. Their resourcefulness and the 'fruitfulness of the country, it being the garden of Ireland with commodious harbours open to France and Spain', meant a revival of trade with those countries. Two of the principal import commodities were weapons and gunpowder. William Saxey, Chief Justice of Munster, reported that the profits were 'sixpence for one penny', enough in his estimation to 'stop the searcher's mouth' – presumably an allusion to the bribery of officials.

THE SPANISH ARMADAS
BACKGROUND

By the middle of the 16th century, England had become a great naval power, in direct opposition to Spain and Portugal, which had divided the New World (North and South America) between them by a treaty, signed in 1494. England and Spain were trading peacefully up to around the 1560s when engagements between English and Spanish ships brought war closer, although publicly the countries were at peace. Part of England's navy was a group of 'privateers', pirates operating under royal, if clandestine, permission. The most famous was Francis Drake, who captured a Spanish treasure ship in 1592 con-

taining 26 tons of silver and 360,000 pieces of gold. This was an immense fortune, part of which Drake kept, as well as obtaining a knighthood. The following year, Sir Walter Raleigh was involved in the taking of a Portuguese ship with over £200,000 worth of silk, jewels, spices and sugar. There were fortunes to be made in those times and England had many men of military and nautical experience to exploit the Atlantic shipping lanes.

A 'Morion', typical Spanish infantryman's helmet of the 16th century.

Gold escudos and a cross of the Order of St James of Santiago, recovered from the wreck of the *Girona*.

Philip II of Spain inherited the Netherlands from his father, Emperor Charles V, in 1555. This region was immensely wealthy from weaving and cloth manufacture. It was also turning Protestant. Philip introduced the Jesuits and the Inquisition, and started burning Protestants at the stake. Elizabeth began helping the Flemish Protestants and, in 1586, English troops landed in the Netherlands.

By 1583, Spain was the most powerful country in Europe, but it was also a wide-ranging force on the high seas. It had looted whole areas of the Americas to the tune of two million ducats per annum, and its navy and army were experienced and formidable. The

Spanish were to the forefront of colonial ambition and Franco Tamara, a cultured Spaniard, described the inhabitants of Haiti as 'vicious, lazy, idle, melancholic, cowardly, base, ungrateful, idolatrous ... with little memory or constancy and given to wicked and abominable sins'. He was referring to the demoralised and psychologically crippled Indians, who had been dispossessed and impoverished. England had no monopoly of colonial contempt.

There were other similarities between the two colonial powers. Both the Spanish and the English considered the 'natives' to be lazy, in that they seemed not to understand the money economy now emerging in Europe as the ideal by which men should live. Aristotle had taught Englishman and Spaniard alike that private possessions made a man work and, therefore, labour for wages would purchase English and Spanish goods, thus creating a market. The Irish and Peruvian had one thing in common, however. Their land was very productive, the abundance it produced creating a leisurely lifestyle, with little need for frantic acquisition. In addition, the kinship ties of common ownership and the lack of a money economy created, in the eyes of the coloniser, a lazy and feckless people.

Some people saw things differently. The Franciscan monk, Father Mendiete, wrote in 1596 of 'the shame which we Christians should feel that pagans of less talent than ourselves should have been better ruled and ordered in matters of morality and behaviour under heathendom, than as Christians under Spanish government'. [Elliot, 2001]

Spain and England shared something else. The 16th century was the beginning of a process of change in how men thought. Authority, long held to be hierarchical and absolute, was yielding to experience, as more sought their fortune outside their native countries. It was colonial expeditions that revealed the importance of opportunity and timing, things that could bring wealth and fame, allowing the lesser sons of the nobility and merchants to acquire the lifestyle that the rich enjoyed at home.

But if the Spanish and the English shared a similar attitude to colonisation and wealth, they diverged on matters of religion. Philip II of Spain had married Mary Tudor, Queen of England, in 1554 and she began a process of attempting to undo the Reformation and began persecuting English Protestants. She died in 1558, remembered bitterly as 'Bloody Mary', although Fort Protector (now Portlaoise) was renamed Maryborough in her honour.

THE GREAT ARMADA

Following the capture of Lisbon in 1580, the Spanish felt strong enough to consider England as a potential prize. Urged on by Philip II, the Marquis of Santa Cruz drew up sea-borne invasion plans of such complexity and cost that even the Spanish treasury and administration, could not manage. The plan, however, appealed to Philip, who, frugal as always, appealed to Pope Sixtus V for money. The Pope promised the enormous sum of one million gold ducats to bring England back to the faith, but when he saw that the Armada was not a fantastic scheme, he became evasive, promising the money if and when the Armada had proved itself a success. Philip scaled down the plans, but remained committed to invading England, using a combination of ships, many of them taken from the Mediterranean, so they were unsuitable for Atlantic seas.

The task of organising the greatest fleet ever seen eventually broke the health and spirit of the Marquis of Santa Cruz, who died in February 1588. The Duke of Medina-Sidonia, reputedly the richest man in Spain, reluctantly took over the vast and under-funded enterprise. Despite delays and incessant problems about money, the invasion fleet was assembled through the commandeering of foreign vessels. The Duke of Parma's army in the Netherlands was ordered to make ready an invasion fleet of barges to cross the North Sea.

The Armada was made up of several mini-fleets, some of which were slow-moving merchant vessels, originally designed to carry Mediterranean grain or bullion from the Americas. Others were galleasses, an innovation of the time being both sail and oar-powered. In total, more than 130 ships assembled at Lisbon and sailed toward La

Coruna. The Armada eventually sailed towards England in a great crescent formation, covering seven miles of sea and, on the morning of 30 July 1588, in the English Channel, it sighted Drake's fleet astern and closing fast. The Spanish waited for the expected clash of ships when they could fight man-to-man on the decks against the heretics, but Frobisher and Drake, with more cannon and faster ships, simply bombarded the Spanish and refused to engage man-to-man.

English firepower was used to pound the Armada at every opportunity and the great fleet, moving slowly to preserve its formation and to protect the troop and supply ships in the centre, was unable to respond. The fleet needed to repair its damage, so it anchored at Calais where Medina-Sidonia decided to request a meeting with the Duke of Parma to decide on tactics. However, the English attacked by sending in old hulks, filled with blazing pitch. This caused immense panic among the Spanish. They cut their anchors and sailed away from the blazing wrecks, several grounding in the unfamiliar shallows.

The scattered Armada regrouped and sailed northwards along the English coast, shadowed by Drake and Frobisher, but its force was spent. At or around 7 August, the sailing instructions were given: no invasion of England, no rendezvous with Parma in the Netherlands. The fleet was to sail home to Spain. Its venture had failed.

Blown northwards by gathering storms, the great fleet sailed around Scotland heading into the north Atlantic and an unforeseen hurricane. Within a week, news reached London that great numbers of galleons had been sighted off the west coast of Ireland. Elizabeth and her court were stunned. Were the Spanish planning to land, join the Irish and fight? They issued proclamations that forbade any help to a Spaniard on pain of death and confiscation of property.

But the fleet was not intending an invasion of Ireland. It was seriously damaged and 23 galleons had turned eastwards towards Ireland, seeking shelter from the weather

A gold reliquary, originally containing candle wax from St Peters, blessed by the Pope possibly belonging to the Bishop of Killaloe, who perished on the Armada galleass *Girona*.

and a shorter route home. Many were pounded to pieces by the storms and shattered against the western seaboard from Donegal to Kerry. Of the thousands of men shipwrecked on Ireland's coast, only one in seven survived. Over 5,000 died on the lonely beaches, killed by the English soldiery or Irish scavengers.

STREEDAGH STRAND, CO. SLIGO

It was along this strand in September 1588 that three galleons of the Spanish Armada were wrecked following a storm. They were blown toward the strand and overturned, spilling men and contents into the surging water. A local official, Sir Geoffrey Fenton, reported to Lord Burleigh, 'I numbered in one strand, less than five miles in length, eleven-hundred dead corpses'. One of those who escaped was Francisco de Cuellar, a 16th-century James Bond, who evaded capture and certain death on the beach and eventually found the castle of McClancy on Lough Gara where he hid. The soldiers tracked him down and McClancy ran off. De Cuellar, however, beat off the soldiers and the chieftain returned, celebrating de Cuellar as a hero and insisting he join the family by marrying his sister. De Cuellar demurred and left that night, but was captured near Sligo town. The soldiers stopped at an inn to celebrate his arrest and de Cuellar appeared downcast and submissive. He persuaded a 'wench' to amuse his captors and climbed out a back window and got away. He eventually escaped to Scotland and thence to Spain, to tend his orange groves and reminisce about Ireland.

In the spring of 1596, Philip II committed himself to support Ireland again. Alonzo de Cobros was sent from Santander with enough gold and ammunition to supply the army of O'Neill and O'Donnell for 18 months. Philip also sent two Spanish officers, captains Cisneros and Mendinilla, to train the northern armies, liaise with the chieftains and reconnoitre the coast for a suitable landing place. De Cobos returned from Spain to Killybegs in September 1596 and met the assembled chiefs of Ulster at a great conference held in

Donegal Castle. It was decided that the expedition from Spain should land at Carlingford or Galway. Philip II gathered a great Armada for Ireland at Cadiz in October 1596, consisting of 98 galleons, 10,800 men and many Irish soldiers. They sailed toward Cape Finisterre with the sounds of the psalm Contra Paganos, sung by the choir of Cadiz Cathedral, wafting from the quayside.

Silver escudos and gold sovereigns recovered from Armada wrecks.

As before, Spain was unlucky at sea and a great storm scattered the Armada for Ireland and dispersed the ships. It was to be a year before everything could be gathered again and, by that time, Tyrone and his forces were weakening.

However, Spain under the Olivares was occupied with the expulsion of the Moriscos from Valencia, Aragon and Catalonia. Almost two-thirds were Christian and there were worries that their children would relapse into Islam. Proposals were put forward to retain the children as slaves to Christian families, thereby retaining their faith, if not their freedom. In the end, an estimated 400,000 individuals were deported to the North African coast as 'Moors'. Their fate was known in advance and most died from the predicted starvation. Like the expulsion of the Huguenots from France, the country suffered. The Moriscos, like the Huguenots, were an intellectual and mercantile middle class, contributing in no small way to the 'success' of the state in which they lived. Spain still had the pillaged bullion from her American colonies to redress the balance, but the 17th century saw the decline of this income and the rise of piracy. Spain declined throughout this era and its monarchy, if judged by the brushwork of Velasquez, appeared to be a combination of indolence, piety and debauchery. [Ogg, 1932]

THE FINAL STRUGGLE

The medieval period came to an end for Ireland in the troubled times of the late 16th century. It was when Gaelic Ireland went under, led by a man whose personal ambitions reached beyond what was possible at the time. The Nine Years War was the last struggle of Gaelic Ireland against England where the forces were at least reasonably matched but it became the curtain call for that culture of opposition. The demise of Gaelic Ireland is largely the story of Hugh O'Neill and his dream of being Lord of Ireland, with Spanish help.

O'Neill's vision of an island – Catholic certainly, Spanish perhaps – was based on an assumption that religion alone could be a badge of unity, pulling together the Catholic 'Old English' of great families and townspeople under a banner held aloft by an Ulster prince. But the idea of Hugh O'Neill as Lord of Ireland did not merit unanimous support across all sections of the population, whatever their religious persuasion. The towns remained independent of all, but loyal to the Crown while many in Munster remembered O'Neill's support of Lord Deputy Sidney during the Desmond Wars. During those terrible years, ruthless English captains burned Munster from end to end, vying with each other's progress by the parallel burning of cabins along the southern peninsulas. [O'Faoláin, 1945]

Such a belief in religion as a unifying force was itself a medieval idea, as was his assumption that he was the greatest of men, with absolute rights over his territory. It was as if he was unaware of the fate of other 'over-mighty subjects' earlier in the century, particularly the FitzGeralds of Kildare and Desmond, in whose destruction he had participated. The contemporary chieftains of Connacht were certainly not of his quality and failed to outmanœuvre Bingham, the governor, who was a roaring bloodthirsty individual, incapable of subtlety and compromise. Those who survived submitted. Likewise, the chief families of Leix (Laois) and Offaly were provoked into rebellion and, by the middle of the century, were exiled and their lands taken.

Despite the reluctance of many to support him, O'Neill comes across as suave, complex and dangerous, a man with one smouldering ambition – to drive the English, bag and baggage, out of Ireland with whatever help he could get. Without doubt, he was a man of considerable resources, agreeing a rate of six cows for one musket with the merchants of Cork, while his secret agent smuggled gunpowder into Ireland in barrels marked 'Best English Beer'. The Irish soldiers under his command were perhaps the most patriotic ever to fight against England. Under O'Neill, they were not fighting for a tribe or even for a king. They were fighting for Ireland. It was reported in London, 'by strong hand they intend to regain the kingdom for themselves'... and in O'Neill's words, 'so that the island of Ireland shall be at our direction and council as Irishmen'. For despite his English education in the Pale outside Dublin, O'Neill remained committed to his own dynastic ambitions and his greater vision. As to the skills required, he was a superb military commander and an organiser of genius. [Hayes-McCoy, 1969]

An Ireland independent of England through military victory was no idle dream as Philip of Spain sent officers to train O'Neill's men and money to pay them. The Irish now had an army ready to join the Spanish if they would come. But the stakes were getting higher in this game of political poker between Elizabeth and O'Neill. Pardons and treaties were offered and considered, for if Hugh won, Ireland would be under Spanish royal control, with him as Philip's Irish 'king'. The island would be resolutely Catholic, and ready to assist in the invasion of heretic England. Ireland slowly became England's Cuba, a hostile offshore island, armed and supported by a dangerous foreign power. Hugh O'Neill had moved his country from being a nuisance to being an enemy.

Although losing an important battle with the failure of the 1588 Armada and the generally appalling treatment of survivors on Ireland's coast, Spain seemed intent on using Ireland to attack England again and reinstate Catholicism. The espousal of the Catholic cause, while perhaps expedient from Hugh O'Neill's point of view, endeared him to King Philip of Spain, Pope Clement's champion. In Ireland, the Counter-Reformation, a movement for the restoration and reform of that religion, brought a holy zeal to the internal struggles and defined nationality in religious terms, perhaps for the first time.

The Spanish sent further Armadas in 1596 and 1597, each carrying 10,000 troops, an army that would have seriously challenged England's capacity to hold Ireland, but both were wrecked by storms. Undeterred, O'Neill petitioned for further help and played for time. His espousal of Catholicism and Spain, however, moved him from being a mighty subject seeking absolute authority in his own territory to becoming a mortal enemy of England and Protestant Elizabeth I. In retrospect, this conflict of his choosing ultimately brought the profound changes in Ulster that would last to the present day. O'Neill chose the feudal past instead of the pragmatic future and Ulster paid the price for his defeat. [Morgan, 2004]

His campaign began with notable victories such as the Battle of Clontibret in County Monaghan in May 1595. While not suffering serious casualties or a defeat in any great sense, it was a huge shock to the confidence of Elizabethan England. It happened because of the need to relieve the fort at Monaghan, then an isolated garrison in a wilderness of woods and lakes. The Irish tactics of attack and withdrawal were used to great effect, constantly harrying a long column on the march, attacking and inflicting casualties before the slower-moving enemy could regroup to defend themselves. The same tactics would result in a serious defeat for the English in 1598.

THE BATTLE OF THE YELLOW FORD

On a warm August day in 1598 the veterans marching in the English army sent to relieve the fort on the Blackwater felt confident in their 4,000 infantry and cavalry, led by Marshal Bagenal. They had a six-mile hike from their Armagh camp to the fort and set off like a great parade, drums beating and flags waving, their slow-moving supply wagons and artillery pulled by teams of bullocks. They were in three divisions, well armed and had but a short march ahead. The first group set off wide of the narrow track to the fort and within a short distance, 1,200 men and horses had ploughed the ground into a muddy morass. The middle group with the supply wagons fell behind and a distance of some 130 yards opened up between each of the three groups.

Hugh O'Neill, Earl of Tyrone and military strategist, was waiting. He had been joined by the soldiers of Maguire, O'Donnell, O'Rourke, MacDonnell and Burke. They could see the English coming, their army now stretched into an enormous colourful snake, nearly half-a-mile long. But before the Irish fought, they dug. Even today, the ground between the site of the English camp and the fort is crisscrossed with ancient ditches, deep and difficult to cross, forcing the individual or an army in certain directions and impeding free movement.

At a point two miles north of Armagh, the leading third of Bagenal's army met a huge water-filled trench, five feet deep and four wide, stretching half-a-mile in either direction, between bogs

and woods. It lay in front of an intermeshed thorny strategic   barricade, blocking the route forward. Then the sniping began in earnest. Irish musketeers, hidden in the trees, had intermittently attacked Bagenal's army, but now in a deadly fusillade, they shot officers, horses, soldiers and the bullocks that pulled the deadly cannon. The artillery was abandoned and the middle of the army, out of sight from the front, stalled in confusion. Men were dying by the minute from sharpshooters, when the Irish cavalry attacked, hacking into the demoralised infantry. Whole sections of the English army were annihilated.

Some 300 Irish mercenaries in Bagenal's army deserted to O'Neill, leaving the English army widely separated, pinned down by sharpshooters and deadly pike attacks. The leading group pressed on and crossed the great ditch, but seeing that they were separated from the main army, began a retreat, only to receive a full attack from O'Neill's army. Bagenal himself rode up, attempting to rally the troops by lifting the visor on his helmet. He was killed instantly by a bullet to the head from an Irish marksman. Then a powder barrel exploded and a rout began. The Irish cavalry and infantry continued to attack along the column, leaving 1,500 of Elizabeth's soldiers dead on the battlefield. It was the greatest Irish victory for centuries and the worst English defeat in Ireland.

Now all O'Neill needed was the Spanish and Ireland could be his. It was to be three years before they landed and then in small numbers. Spanish soldiers eventually landed 200 miles away – in Kinsale. The final battle for Gaelic Ireland was about to take place.

KINSALE

By the time Hugh O'Neill reached the outskirts of Kinsale in 1601, he and his army had won three battles against the Elizabethans, out-manœuvred the Earl of Essex in his campaign, considered and rejected a pardon and submission to Elizabeth, and generally imposed his will on a considerable portion of the island. Munster, however, had been the subject of a continuing campaign by Lord Mountjoy and was no longer capable of fighting on O'Neill's behalf.

For the first time, strategic leadership, the Irish Cause and a real army all stood together. O'Neill's army was the first to have its own drums and colours – red coats, given to him when his army was 'Loyal' – and be capable of drilling in the English fashion under proper field officers. It was a force to be reckoned with. The opinion of the time was that if O'Neill and his Spanish allies could take Munster, Ireland could be won.

Elizabeth and her ministers realised the nature of this desperate struggle and she made sure that Mountjoy, her most skilled general, was aware of his task. Up to this point, strategy, the skill of the military leader, had been O'Neill's greatest strength, when in previous fights caution and tactics had won the day. Previously, he had fought the English using Ulster's bogs and mountains as allies, but now he was 200 miles from his natural terrain, in the strange country of Munster, and the Spaniards, holed up in Kinsale, were not under his direct command. There were no bogs and woods to hide in.

By the time O'Neill arrived outside Kinsale on 21 December 1601, the Spanards had been under siege for almost ten weeks and were weary of Ireland. Admiral Leveson was blockading them in the harbour. The majority of the (English) army opposite them was composed of Catholic Irish, the very people they were supposed to save, and the Catholic inhabitants of Munster were unwilling to help them in their plight. Low on supplies and short on patience, their commander, Don Juan del Aquila, urged O'Neill by secret letter to attack the English according to a plan he had devised.

On his march south, O'Neill had been joined by O'Donnell, O'Boyle, MacSweeney, O'Conor-Roe, MacDermot, O'Kelly and some of the O'Flahertys. The Knight of Glin and FitzMaurice of Kerry joined his force. All in all, the army of Hugh O'Neill was perhaps 6,000 men and 500 horse (cavalry) with a further 300 Spaniards at Castlehaven under the command of Zubiar, a Basque admiral. Inside the walls were some 3,000 Spaniards. Although the sides seemed equal in numbers, the English were suffering from disease and starvation and many of its Irish recruits were deserting. Mountjoy considered retiring to Cork and lifting the siege if O'Neill decided to dig in but Don Juan del Aquila had developed a personal enmity toward the Irish at this stage and, perhaps in order to bring things to a finish, urged an attack, to be co-ordinated with his forces in the town.

On the night of 23 December, a frightful storm broke over both armies as the Irish forces unhappily complied with del Aquila's plan and made their way to a hill overlooking the English camp. By the time they arrived, O'Donnell's troops were far behind, but the English, far from being surprised, were ready and mounted. According to rumour, they had been forewarned by a renegade MacMahon. O'Neill's men were tired and soaking wet and in no order for fighting a battle on open ground. Despite their victories in previous years, they had never fought except as ambushers and skirmishers. There was hesitation in the Irish command and the troops waited in groups for instructions. At this moment, the English cavalry attacked and the Irish wavered. For an hour they held off the cavalry and despite O'Neill's bravery and command, they broke and fled the field. By the time O'Donnell arrived, it was too late. He attempted to rally the troops but a headlong retreat had begun and the army of Ulster was in disarray. At least 1,000 were killed outright on the field and no prisoners were taken. Any wounded or surrendered men were hanged immediately. The wounded Spanish were driven into Kinsale to weaken whatever supplies were left in the town.

Confusion is what comes across from the shambles that was the Battle of Kinsale. Admiral Zubiar, a veteran naval commander, kept his troops at Castlehaven, away from the battle. O'Neill and O'Donnell were not of one mind as to tactics, the Irish cavalry were mounted on small horses, incapable of withstanding an English cavalry charge, and the Irish were the wrong army for the job. The English won a huge victory, with the loss of less than a dozen men. The Irish army was shattered, leaving another 800 dead through wounds and subsequent panic-stricken flight. The Irish believed the Spanish in the town of Kinsale to be cowardly, while Don Juan, expressing supreme contempt for the Irish, surrendered on honorable terms and became a close friend of Sir George Carew. The Spanish left and sailed back to Spain. They would not help Ireland again.

FINALE

Perhaps the saddest item of this wretched chapter of Irish history is the secret murder of Hugh O'Neill's son, Henry. He was a page, or really a hostage, with the Archduke Albert in Brussels and was Hugh's future hope. He was found strangled in 1617, the year after Hugh's death, murdered, it was believed, by agents of the crown keen to prevent any further 'O'Neill' from attempting to take power in Ulster. But if Hugh had supported, or at least compromised with, the Queen, it is unlikely that Ulster would have been planted. There would not have been the tragic history that we are all so familiar with. But he chose the past instead of the future, the Gaelic world instead of the Queen's world. In pitting Ulster against London, he lost. But in forcing the Queen to carry through a policy of military conquest, he turned what could have been a forgotten part of Irish history into a living memory. And it instilled in the victors of Ulster, and its subsequent plantation, a lingering fear of retaliation from the dispossessed which forever denied them the fruits of their conquest.

Conclusions and Loss

T HE COST OF THE Elizabethan conquest was calculated at the vast sum of £1,500,000 sterling in 1601. [Black, 1937] Ireland was at peace, subjugated, and economically destroyed. The Elizabethans succeeded, however, in attaching the Irish people more than ever to the Catholic Church and Rome, their religious belief becoming the only piece of identity that could not be taken and sold. Politically, Ulster was to be planted, Connacht was submissive, while the trade of Munster never recovered its earlier productivity and its natural timber resources were sold off. Elizabethan England was the State at War, a unitary, forceful willing of a particular viewpoint, Nationalism, at its most brutal and intolerant.

AN ADVENTURER

It can be difficult to visualise the extent of plantations in their millions of acres, but one particularly vivid individual can give a picture of the many adventurers who came to Ireland to exploit its riches and profit by its downfall. In 1588, Richard Boyle arrived in Ireland with £27 sterling, a diamond ring and the clothes he stood up in. By the time he died in 1644, he was probably the richest man in Ireland. He bought Raleigh's estate at Lismore, exported the timber and established iron works, using the remaining oak from the forests of the Blackwater to smelt the ingots. He stripped hundreds of thousands of trees from the old monastic lands and acquired other lands across Munster. The timber was then floated down the Blackwater to Youghal. Ultimately he exported 20,000 quarters of timber for barrel staves from Youghal, each quarter being worth around £1,000 sterling at that time.

LANGUAGE AND CULTURE

If one were to extract one thing from the end of Medieval Ireland, something that was never recovered, unlike the land and independence, it would be the language. Up to the dispossessions and confiscations in the Elizabethan period and later, Ireland still had something unique; the vast privacy of a different language; something inscrutable, foreign, not to be penetrated quickly or easily.

The Elizabethan poet and adventurer Edmund Spenser spent several years in Ireland and argued that the Irish language, Gaelic, was subversive, being a reminder of difference and separateness. He wrote:

> the wordes are the image of the mynde, so as they proceeding from the mynde must bee needes affected with the wordes: So that the speech beinge Irish, the harte must needes bee Irishe, for out of the aboundance of the harte the tongue speaketh.
>
> [LEERSEN, 1996]

In other words, if the people are speaking Irish, then Irish they must be. The language was more than a grammar, a syntax of expression. It was an internal guide to external reality.

By 1690, the Irish were dispossessed of their lands and the social aspect of their society. English was forcibly introduced as the language of law, property, and governance. As the English language permeated firstly the official discourse, then education and then the vernacular, great numbers of the Irish people gradually became anglicised. Finally, Irish ceased to be the discourse of poetry. That language, formerly spoken by as many people in Ireland as Danish in the Baltic region, declined. Irish had offered cohesiveness within the island between Celt, Norseman and Norman and, like Christianity before the

Reformation, it was a discourse that could be shared. Perhaps it was the ultimate core of Irish identity itself.

Burncourt Castle, Co. Tipperary, built by Sir Richard Everard and burnt by Cromwell in 1650. It was never rebuilt.

The language continued its decline until it became the language of the landless peasantry. It had an aristocratic ghost life, its poetic *deibhidhe agus setna*, rhyme and metre, reappearing in later Latin psalms. [Carney, 1967] By the 1700s, the language was for many a hindrance to prosperity. At the very least, it was a reminder of the past and a defeated past at that. By the time Irish republicanism was born in 1789, it spoke English.

For Ireland, as for all nations, the state ultimately decides what History is; over time it chooses what is to be included in the *Great Narrative of the People*. In Ireland's case, that story revolved around rural Ireland of the 19th century, those who remained speaking the Irish language, the designated carriers of an ancient culture. What they represented was not the remnants of Medieval Ireland or the great struggles against Elizabethan England, but the idealisation, indeed fetishisation of one group of people whose interests were represented by those who came to power, principally in 1932.

The long colourful tapestry of Irish Medieval history was

replaced as a cultural resource by a sentimental rural narrative, an *imposed* memory for all. As a people, we gradually became that imagined history through its telling and gradual integration through the educational system and the arts. These mythic simplifications of true identity found their way into economic policy and an entire cultural outlook was created, based on a romantic dream of pastoral life that ignored both the complexity of Irish history and the contemporary poverty and emigration behind its façade.

The simplistic and nationalist history of 1916, Cromwell and Brian Ború was maybe an attempt not so much to understand the past as to explain why we found ourselves in the position we did. Medieval history, with its paradox, splits and differing loyalties, was just too complicated for the Irish identity that was being created after Independence.

So what do we learn from Medieval Ireland now, what can we take from that time?

It did not have a unitary character and was almost a kind of pluralist society, in opposition to Elizabethan 'nationalism', the domination of one state, one language, one culture over all others. Ireland, in a curious way, was ahead of its time for all its split loyalties, problems and paradoxes. It was a society of many identities and allegiances, sharing both a common language and in the early period at least, religious belief.

The people of Ireland today are, in a cultural sense at least, the inheritors of that medieval world in all its complexity, colour and uniqueness. We as a people are not the long-lost offspring of a mystic Celtic realm, but the flesh and blood descendants of Celts (maybe), Romans (perhaps), Anglo-Saxons (possibly), but definitely Vikings, Normans, Elizabethans and Scots all of which make up what is Irishness. Medieval Ireland may yet show how the many can live within the wide parameters of a shared tradition, because surely, we are the children of all our history and knowing that story with its sometimes hurtful truth and many uncertainties is infinitely better than a mythology that ignores the past.

Bibliography

The Rooney Library at the American College, Dublin
Ballymun Public Library
The Journal of the Royal Society of Antiquaries

Arnold, Bruce, *A Concise History of Irish Art*, Thames & Hudson, 1969
Barrington, T.J., *Discovering Kerry*, Blackwater Press, 1976
Barry, Terry, *A History of Settlement in Ireland*, Routledge, 2000
Black, J.R.R., *The Reign of Elizabeth, 1558-1603*, Oxford, 1936
Bloch, Marc, *Feudal Society*, Vol I & II, Routledge & Keegan Paul, 1975
Brady, C. & R Gillespie, [eds] *Natives & Newcomers*, Irish Academic Press, 1986
Breffny de, Brian & R ffolliott, *The Houses of Ireland*, Thames & Hudson, 1975
Breffny de, Brian & George Mott, *Churches & Abbeys of Ireland*, Thames & Hudson, 1976
Byrne, Francis J. *Irish Kings and High Kings*, Four Courts Press, 1973
Carney, James, *Medieval Irish Lyrics*, Dolmen Press, 1967
Chadwick, Nora, *The Celts*, Pelican Books, 1979
—— *The Age of the Saints in the Early Celtic Church*, Riddell Memorial Lectures, 1963
Chambers, Anne, *Granuaile*, Wolfhound Press, 1988
—— *Eleanor, Countess of Desmond*, Wolfhound Press, 1986
—— *Chieftain to Knight*, Tibbott Bourke, 1586-1629, Wolfhound Press, 1983
Clarke, Grahame, *Archaeology & Society*, Methuen & Co, 1963
Connolly, S.J., *The Oxford Companion to Irish History*, Oxford University Press, 1998
Connors, Sean, *Mapping Ireland*, Mercier Press, 2001
Cooney G and E. Grogan, *Irish Pre-History*, Wordwell, 1994
Cosgrove, Art, *Late Medieval Ireland, 1350-1541*, Helicon, 1981
Cunliffe, Barry, *Facing the Ocean*, Oxford, 2001
Cunningham, Bernadette, *The World of Geoffrey Keating*, Four Courts Press, 2000
Curtis, Edmund, *A History of Ireland*, Methuen, 1955
Davis, H.W.C., *England under the Normans, 1066-1272*, Methuen, 1945
de Paor, Liam and Maire, *Early Christian Ireland*, Thames & Hudson, 1958
de Breffny, Brian & George Mott, *Churches & Abbeys of Ireland*, Thames & Hudson, 1976
Dillon, Myles, *Early Irish Literature*, University of Chicago Press, 1948
Dolley, Michael, *Anglo-Norman Ireland*, 1100-1318, Gill & Macmillan, 1972
Dronke, Peter, *Women Writers of the Middle Ages*, Cambridge University Press, 1991
Dudley-Edwards, Ruth, *Atlas of Irish History*, Routledge, 1973
Duffy, Sean, [ed] *Atlas of Irish History*, Gill & MacMillan, 1997
Duffy, Sean, *Ireland in the Middle-Ages,* Gill & MacMillan, 1997
Duignan Michael, & Lord Killanin, *Ireland*, [Shell] Ebury Press, 1967
Eco, Umberto, *Art & Beauty in the Middle Ages*, Yale University Press, 1986
Elliott, Marianne, *The Catholics of Ulster*, Penguin Press, 2001

Ellis, Steven, Tudor Ireland, *Crown Community & Conflict of Cultures*, Longman, 1985

Evans, Estyn, *Prehistoric and Early Christian Ireland*, Batsford, 1966

Fisher, H.A.L. *History of Europe*, Arnold, 1936

Flower, Robin, *The Irish Tradition*, Lilliput Press, 1994

Frame, Robin, *English Lordship in Ireland*, 1318-1361, Clarendon Press, 1981

Fraser, Antonia, *The Middle Ages*, Cassell & Co., 2000

Freyne de, Seán, *The Great Silence*, Mercier Press, 1965

Greene, D. and Frank O'Connor, *Irish Poetry, AD 600 to 1200*, Macmillan, 1967

Harbison, Peter, *Pre-Christian Ireland*, Thames & Hudson, 1988

Harbison, Peter, *A Guide to the National Monuments of Ireland*, Gill & Macmillan, 1970 & 1992

Harbison, Peter, Homan Potterton & Jeanne Sheehy, *Irish Art & Architecture,* Thames & Hudson, 1978

Haverty, Martin, *The History of Ireland*, Duffy & Co., Dublin, 1860

Hayes-McCoy, GA, *A Military History of Ireland*, Longmans, 1969.

—— *The Irish at War*, Mercier Press, 1964

Henry, Françoise, *Irish Art in the Early Christian Period*, Methuen, 1940.

Herity, M. and G. Eogan, *Ireland in Prehistory*, Routledge, 1997

Huzinga, J, *The Waning of the Middle Ages*, Harmondworth, 1965

Hyde, Douglas, *Early Gaelic Literature*, Fisher & Unwin, 1923

Jackson, Kenneth, *The Oldest Irish Tradition*, Cambridge University Press, 1964

Kearney, Richard *Postnationalist Ireland*, Routledge, 1997

Kelly, Fergus, *Early Irish Farming*, Dublin Institute for Advanced Studies, 2000

Knopf, A., *Treasures of Irish Art*, Metropolitan Museum of Art, 1999

Leask, Harold, *Irish Churches and Monastic Buildings*, (2 vols) Dundalgan Press, 1955

Leask, Harold, *Irish Castles*, Dundalgan Press, 1972

Leerson, Joep, *Mere Irish and Fíor-Ghael*, Field Day Essays, Cork University Press, 1996

Lydon, James, *Ireland in the Later Middle Ages*, Gill & Macmillan, 1973

MacCurtain, Margaret, *Tudor & Stuart Ireland*, Gill & Macmillan, 1972

McCorristine, Laurence, *The Revolt of Silken Thomas*, Wolfhound Press, 1987

McDonagh, Thomas, *Literature in Ireland*, Talbot Press, 1914

McEneaney, Eamonn, *Waterford City Guide*, O'Brien Press, 2001

——*Waterford Treasures*, [Waterford Museum Publ:] 2004

McEvedy, Colin, *Atlas of Medieval History*, Penguin Press, 1983

MacGeoghegan, Abbe, *The History of Ireland*, James Duffy, 1844

MacNeill, Eoin, *Phases of Irish History*, Gill & Co, 1920

Mac Niocaill, G., *Ireland before the Vikings*, Gill & Macmillan, 1972

Maxwell, C., *Irish History from Contemporary Sources*, Allen & Unwin, 1923

Mitchell, Frank, *The Landscape of Ireland*, Collins Press, 1976

Moody, T. W., *The Londonderry Plantation*, *1609-1641*, Mullan & Son, 1939

Morgan, Hiram, *The Battle of Kinsale*, Wordwell Ltd, 2004

Nicholas, David, *The Evolution of the Medieval World*, Longman, 1992

Nicholls, Kenneth, *Gaelic and Gaelicised Ireland in the Middle Ages*, Gill & Macmillan, 1973

Myers, A.R., *England in the Late Middle Ages*, Pelican, 1952

O'Connor, F and D. Greene, *Treasury of Irish Poetry*, Macmillan, 1967

O'Connor, Frank, *The Backward Look*, Macmillan & Co., 1967

O'Corrain, D., *Ireland before the Vikings*, Gill & Macmillan, 1972

O'Croinin, Daibhi, *Early Medieval Ireland*, Longman, London, 1995

O'Cronin, Risteard, *A History of the O'Deas* Ballinakella Press, 1992

OtwayRuthven, AJ, *A History of Medieval* Ireland, Barnes & Noble, 1980

O'Grady, Standish, *Essays and Passages*, Talbot Press, 1918

Ogg, David, *Europe in the Seventeenth Century*, Black & Co., 1943

O'hOgain, Daithi, *The Sacred Isle*, Boydell Press, 1999

O'Neill, Timothy, *The Irish Hand*, Dolmen Press, 1984

O'Riordain, Seán P., *Antiquities of the Irish Countryside*, Methuen, London 1966

Pochin-Mould, Daphne, *The Mountains of Ireland*, Batsford, 1955

—— *The Monasteries of Ireland*, Batsford, 1976

Pearson, Peter, *The Ancient Heart of Dublin*, O'Brien Press, 2002

Power, Eileen, *Medieval Women*, Cambridge University Press, 1992

Pirenne, H, *Economic History of Medieval Europe*, Kegan Paul, 1936

Rees, E., *Celtic Saints in their Landscape*, Sutton Publishing, 2001

Rhys, John, *Celtic Literature*, SPCK, London, 1904

Richardson, H. and J. Scarry, *Irish High Crosses*, Mercier Press, 1990

Roche, Richard, *The Norman Invasion of Ireland*, Anvil Books, 1970

Roy, James Charles, *The Road Wet, The Wind Close*, Gill & Macmillan, 1986

Smyth, Alfred P. (ed.), *Seanchas. Essays in Honour of Francis Byrne*. Four Courts Press, 2000

Somerville-Large, Peter *From Bantry Bay to Leitrim*, Victor Gollancz, 1980

—— *Dublin* Hamish Hamilton, 1979

—— *Irish Eccentrics,* Hamish Hamilton, 1975

Spellissy, Seán, *Limerick, the Rich Land*, Spellissy & O'Brien, 1989

Stephens, James, *Irish Fairy Tales*, Macmillan & Co., 1923

—— *In the Land of Youth*, Macmillan & Co., 1924

Stopford-Green, Alice, *The Making of Ireland and its Undoing*, Macmillan & Co. London, 1908

Stout, Matthew, *The Irish Ringfort*, Dolmen Press, 1997

Wallace, P.F, *The Architecture of Medieval Dublin* (Comparative History of Urban Organisation in non-Roman Europe), Oxford, 1995

Wallace P.F. and R. O'Floinn, *Treasures of the National Museum*, Gill & Macmillan, 2002

Walsh, Paul, *The Placenames of Westmeath*, Dublin Institute for Advanced Studies, 1957

Ward, A.W and G.W Protheroe, *Cambridge Modern History*, Vol 1-3, Cambridge, 1904

Warner, R., 1976, '*Some observations on the context and importation of exotic material in Ireland, from the first century BC to the second century, AD.* PRIA 76c, 267-292

Warner, R, 1991, '*Cultural Intrusion in the early Iron Age; some notes*' Emania 9 1991 p 44-52

Warner, R., '*Tuathal Techtmar: Myth or ancient literary evidence for a Roman invasion?*' Emania, 13, 1994, p 23-32

Williams, Norman Lloyd, *Sir Walter Raleigh*, Cassell Biographies, 1962

Winnecott, D.W., *Transitional Objects and Potential Spaces*, Columbia University Press, 1993

Index

Plunkett, Edward (Sheriff of
    Meath) 164
Poer, Arnold le (Chief Steward)
    108–10
poetry, Irish 75–6
poets, Irish 76, 111, 164
Poitiers, battle of 133
Poitiers, battle of 133
politics, English 73–4
politics, medieval 133–55
    12th century 59–70
    13th century 70–4, 126,
        131–2, 133–5, 141
    14th century 74, 126–31,
        135–8, 141
    15th century 138–9, 139–41
    16th century 141–55
Pontefract castle, England 137
population figures 41, 87, 102
ports, trading 57
Portugal 168
potato, arrival of 76
pottery 40
Poynings, Sir Edward 140
prices, produce 88
procession, Corpus Christi 95–7
Protestantism 148, 150, 169, 170
Ptolemy's map (of Ireland) 12,
    15–16, 35
pubs, Dublin 98, 101

Q
Quin Abbey, County Clare 50–1

R
Raftery, Professor Barry 37
Raleigh, Walter 76, 167, 168, 169
Raphoe, Bishop of 53–4
Rathangan, County Kildare 111
Rath Breasil, synod of 59
Rathlin Island, County Antrim 55,
    128
Rath Torcaill, Blessington, County
    Dublin 57
Rathurles, County Tipperary
    ring-fort 18

redshanks 104, 125
Reformation 141, 142, 145–55, 160,
    170, 178
reformation movement 31, 48
reformers, church 53
refugees 16
relics 45, 49
religion. see Catholicism;
    Christianity; paganism; papacy;
    Protestantism
reliquary, gold 172
rent, black 123, 168
rent collectors 43
Revenue Commissioners 117
Reynolds, Charles (Archbishop of
    Kells) 162
Richard-an-Iarainn 153
Richard II, King 95
    and Ireland 135–6, 137
Richard III, King 139
ring-forts 41
Rathurles, County Tipperary 18
Robert the Bruce 127–8, 130–1
Roche, Lord 151
Roche, Prior Milo 81–2
Roche, Richard FitzGodbert de
    63
Roche, William 54
Rockfleet Castle, Clew Bay,
    County Mayo 105
Rock of Cashel County Tipperary
    21–2
Roman Empire 35–7, 45, 46
Romanesque heads 163
Roscommon, County 116–17
Rufus, King 57

S
St Aubyn, Adam 135
St Aubyns 134
St Benedict 77–8
St Bernard 59
St Brigid's Cathedral 84
St Canice's Cathedral 67
St Ciaran 76

St Colmcille 48
St Coman 116, 117
St Comgall 80
St Cyril of Alexandria 49
St David, Menavia, Wales
St Declan 46
St Dorothy 78
St Edmund 86
St Fiacre 78
St Francis 114
St Gaelasus 60
St Laurence's Gate, Drogheda,
    County Louth 20
St Leger, Sir Anthony 142
St Mary de Hogge 93
St Mary's Abbey 97–8, 159–60
St Mary's Cathedral, Limerick
    carvings 159
St Mo Lua 80
St Mullins, Kilkenny 57
St Ninian, Whithorn, Scotland 47
St Patrick 35, 45, 46
St Patrick's Cathedral, Dublin 95,
    142
St Patrick's University, Dublin 82,
    84
St Tola 131
St Wolstan 79
Salisbury, John of 59
San Joseph, Colonel 167
Santa Cruz, Marquis of 171
Saxey, William (Chief Justice of
    Munster) 168
Scarborough Castle 74
schools 81–3, 86. see also colleges;
    universities
Scotland 30–1
    freedom 74
Scots 30–1
Seals, royal 136, 152
settlements
    Roman 37–40
    Romanised Britons 16
    Viking 48, 56–7, 91–3, 94–5
Shetland Islands 56